Catching Up: What LDCs can do, and how others can help

Paul Collier

COMMONWEALTH SECRETARIAT

Commonwealth Secretariat
Marlborough House, Pall Mall
London SW1Y 5HX, United Kingdom

© Commonwealth Secretariat 2011

All rights reserved. No part of this publication may be reproduced, stored in a retrieval system, or transmitted in any form or by any means, electronic or mechanical, including photocopying, recording or otherwise without the permission of the publisher.

Published by the Commonwealth Secretariat
Edited and designed by Wayzgoose
Cover design by Tattersall Hammarling & Silk
Index by Indexing Specialists (UK) Ltd
Printed by Charlesworth Press

Views and opinions expressed in this publication are the responsibility of the author and should in no way be attributed to the Commonwealth Secretariat.

Wherever possible, the Commonwealth Secretariat uses paper sourced from sustainable forests or from sources that minimise a destructive impact on the environment.

Copies of this publication may be obtained from

The Publications Section
Commonwealth Secretariat, Marlborough House
Pall Mall, London SW1Y 5HX
United Kingdom
Tel: +44 (0)20 7747 6534
Fax: +44 (0)20 7839 9081
Email: publications@commonwealth.int
Web: www.thecommonwealth.org/publications

A catalogue record for this publication is available from the British Library.

ISBN: 978-1-84929-051-7 (paperback)
ISBN: 978-1-84859-103-5 (downloadable e-book)

About the author

Paul Collier is Professor of Economics and Director of the Centre for the Study of African Economies at Oxford University. He is the author of *The Bottom Billion: Why the Poorest Countries are Failing and What Can be Done About It* (Oxford University Press, 2007).

Contents

Foreword		vii
Abbreviations		xi
1	Introduction	1
2	The Challenge of Natural Resource Exploitation	5
3	Using Trade Preferences to Help LDCs Break into Global Manufacturing	19
4	Regional Integration	35
5	Innovations in Financing Development	43
6	Climate Change, Asian Growth and Food Security in LDCs	59
7	Conclusion	67
References		73
Index		75

Foreword

Least Developed Countries (LDCs) have been recognised as a category of states that are highly disadvantaged in their development process and face a disproportionate risk of failing to overcome poverty and other consequences associated with weak human resource capacity and economic vulnerability. To help devise responses to the challenges that they face, the United Nations has hosted three special conferences on LDCs. The first two, held in Paris in 1981 and 1991, and the third, held in Brussels in 2001, adopted programmes of action calling for various measures to be undertaken by the international development community to ameliorate the circumstances of LDCs.

At the third UN LDC conference, governments committed themselves to the eradication of poverty in the world's poorest countries. The Brussels Programme of Action for 2001–2010 addressed several key issues, including trade preferences, development assistance and debt cancellation. The most significant outcomes were declarations on the full implementation of debt relief schemes under the heavily indebted poor countries (HIPC) initiative and trade preference programmes, particularly the European Union's (EU) granting of duty free quota free market access for all exports originating in LDCs under its Everything but Arms (EBA) initiative.

During the last decade, LDCs have generally demonstrated an impressive economic performance. In the period 2002–2008, LDCs real gross domestic product (GDP) grew by more than 7 per cent. Despite the global economic slowdown LDCs managed to achieve a modest growth of close to 4 per cent in 2009. Yet serious concerns remain about the depth and sustainability of this notable recent progress, with a range of very significant challenges continuing to confront this group of countries. First, strong and sustained economic growth has bypassed a large number of LDCs and the rate of poverty reduction has been sluggish. A principal LDC objective – of achieving structural transformation – remains elusive. Indeed, the recent export boom from LDCs has been overwhelmingly dominated by primary commodities, while the contribution of manufacturing to output has remained largely unchanged in most LDCs over the past three decades. Moreover, LDCs continue to remain vulnerable to commodity price volatility, so that they have been exposed to repeated external shocks, while a lack of food security continues to present major challenges for a large number of net food-importing LDCs.

Despite making some progress towards improved market access, LDC exports still face significant barriers. The failure to conclude the Doha Round of multilateral trade negotiations sponsored by the World Trade Organization (WTO) has also adversely affected LDC interests in a number of sectors that are of critical importance to them. Similarly, despite an increase in the volume of official development assistance (ODA), most donors have failed to fulfil their aid commitments to LDCs. At the same time, foreign direct investment (FDI) flows have largely been concentrated on a few natural resource rich countries. Multilateral debt relief provided under the Heavily Indebted Poor Countries (HIPC) and Multilateral Debt Relief Initiatives has helped contain debt service payments at manageable levels, but the long-term sustainability of debt remains a daunting challenge for most LDCs. In the meantime, several new challenges have emerged since the third LDC conference in Brussels, including higher food and fuel prices, a significant increase in the economically active populations in LDCs who lack employment opportunities and the impact on LDCs of climate change as a result of global warming. The past decade has also witnessed the increasing global economic power of a number of developing countries, including China, Brazil, India, Russia and South Africa, and their emergence as significant players in global trade and investment flows. Understanding how LDCs can benefit from their economic relations with the affluent South has become an increasingly important issue.

Against this backdrop, the fourth UN LDC conference (LDC-IV) will take place in Istanbul, Turkey, in May 2011. Amongst other objectives, the conference is expected to adopt new measures and strategies to promote the sustainable development of LDCs into the next decade.

The conference is of great interest to the Commonwealth Secretariat, as democracy and development are two fundamental pillars of the Commonwealth's activities. The Secretariat strives to contribute to pro-poor sustainable economic growth in its developing country members. Fifteen of the Commonwealth's 54 members are LDCs, and the Secretariat attaches special priority to the trade and development interests of these countries. Technical assistance in the areas of institutional development, trade policy formulation and implementation, capacity development in a wide range of sectors, and the introduction of new ideas and consensus building in various regional and global initiatives for promoting development-friendly outcomes are the principal means through which the Commonwealth aims to attain its objectives.

Given the importance of LDC-IV, the Secretariat has contributed to the preparatory process in several ways, by providing analytical inputs and supporting the exchange of ideas amongst important stakeholders, including policy-makers, donors, civil society groups and policy experts. It has commissioned a series of analytical papers that address key policy themes for discussion at LDC-IV, and their findings have been presented and discussed in various forums.

I would like to take this opportunity to thank Professor

Paul Collier, who responded enthusiastically to our proposal to write this detailed, interesting and insightful study. Policy-makers and other stakeholders across the Commonwealth will find that the volume is a valuable, welcome and commendable addition to the existing body of knowledge relating both to the understanding of the challenges faced by LDCs and the policy options through which these challenges can be addressed.

I would also like to express my sincere gratitude to CUTS-International for its collaboration in this project and for its technical contributions to developing other related studies.

Cyrus Rustomjee
Director, Economic Affairs Division

Abbreviations

AGOA	African Growth and Opportunity Act
CBI	Caribbean Basin Initiative
CPIA	*Country Policy and Institutional Assessment*
EBA	Everything but Arms
ECOWAS	Economic Community of West African States
EITI	Extractive Industries Transparency Initiative
EME	Emerging market economy
EPA	Economic partnership agreement
EPZ	Export processing zone
EU	European Union
FDI	Foreign direct investment
GDP	Gross domestic product
GM	Genetic modification
GMO	Genetically modified organism
GSP	Generalised System of Preferences
HIPC	Heavily indebted poor countries
IBRD	International Bank for Reconstruction and Development
ICRG	International Country Risk Guide
IDA	International Development Association
IFC	International Finance Corporation
IFI	International finance institution
IMF	International Monetary Fund
LDC	Least developed country
MDRI	Multilateral Debt Relief Initiative
MDG	Millennium development goal
MFA	Multi-fibre Agreement
NGO	Non-governmental organisation
ODA	Official development assistance
OECD	Organisation for Economic Co-operation and Development

PEFA	Public expenditure and financial accountability
PSA	Public service agency
ROO	Rules of origin
SWF	Sovereign wealth fund
UNIDO	United Nations Industrial Development Organization
WTO	World Trade Organization

1   Introduction

The period 2000–2008 was, in retrospect, a remarkable global boom during which developing countries converged rapidly on member countries of the Organisation for Economic Co-operation and Development (OECD). Most least developed countries took part in this growth, in contrast to the previous two decades, during which they had stagnated. Per capita income rose on average by an unprecedented 4 per cent per year, and this was reflected in some of the fundamental indicators of wellbeing: for example, infant mortality dropped by around 11 per cent. Consistent with these impressive improvements in outcomes, measures of governance advanced: assessing governance is controversial, but the average score on the widely-used International Country Risk Guide (ICRG) increased by nearly 4.5 points.

However, despite these solid achievements, on important measures LDCs continued to diverge from the rest of mankind. In other developing countries per capita income rose even faster, by over 5 per cent per year, so the income differential between LDCs and other developing countries widened. In absolute terms, in LDCs per capita income rose by just under US$100, whereas in other developing countries it rose by over US$600. In relative terms, the differential widened from 5.1:1 to 5.4:1. Similarly, in other developing countries infant mortality dropped even more rapidly, by an astonishing 18 per cent. Even in terms of governance, on the ICRG measure, while LDCs advanced absolutely, they did not succeed in closing the gap with other developing countries.

Hence, although there was certainly an improvement in LDC performance during the boom of 2000–2008, there is no basis for complacency. Indeed, the very fact that there is still, in 2010, a group of least developed countries is an indication of serious past failures on the part of both the international

… despite these solid achievements, on important measures least developed countries continued to diverge from the rest of mankind.

The world economy has entered a period of profound and rapid change. LDCs face a new range of challenges and opportunities.

community and the governments of LDCs themselves. There are many policies that could have been effective in enabling LDCs to converge on the economic conditions experienced by the rest of mankind. That these have not been implemented reflects a lack of strategic focus, and a lack of coordination, by key decision takers. The future can and must be different. The world economy has entered a period of profound and rapid change. LDCs face a new range of challenges and opportunities.

Consider an alarming, though by no means inevitable, prospect. Over the next two decades most of the people living in those developing countries already richer than the LDCs rapidly converge on the developed countries. Meanwhile, the LDCs merely repeat their performance of the last two decades. In considering such a prospect a caveat is in order: the membership of the categories of 'LDC' and 'other developing countries' is sure to change somewhat. Already, some of the countries still officially classified as 'least developed' are no longer appropriate for the category. For example, Equatorial Guinea is officially 'least developed', yet as a consequence of oil discoveries it has been one of the most rapidly growing economies in the world and its per capita income is now far above LDC levels. Conversely, a few developing countries that are not currently in the 'least developed' category may become so as a result of misfortune such as conflict, climate change or the exhaustion of natural assets. Nevertheless, accepting that the composition of the categories may change somewhat, the first part of this prospect – the convergence of most other developing countries with the developed economies – is likely to happen. Indeed, over the course of this century most countries other than LDCs (and all the populous ones) are likely to converge sufficiently to be eligible to join the OECD. By 2100 most people will be living in developed countries. A bitter lesson of the post-independence period for LDCs is that growth in the world economy need not imply growth in their own economies. If the rest of the world converges on prosperity, countries that remain in poverty risk becoming increasingly detached. Their brightest young people will aspire to emigrate, and there will be far more countries that are attractive and feasible destinations. As locations for economic activity, the LDCs will increasingly be regarded as suitable only for natural resource extraction.

The future for LDCs need not be like this, but it will be unless there is effective change. The rest of the developing world will rapidly develop; in LDCs business-as-usual will not deliver the substantial acceleration necessary to keep pace with them, let alone to catch up.

Effective change depends in part upon the design of a strategic package of policies: the task is too large for any single policy. It also depends upon co-ordination: the task is too large for any single actor. Finally, it depends upon sustained implementation: the gap between LDCs and the rest of mankind is now so wide that closing it will take decades.

The key reason why this has not happened to date is that LDC governments have not collectively seized the initiative. Instead, the space has been occupied by a growing variety of agencies, none of which has the authority to command a co-ordinated effort.

The only actors who can lead a process of effective change are the governments of LDCs themselves, acting in common. They have the most compelling reason to remain serious and focused. If they took common action to achieve clear and well-founded goals, including implementing those actions within their direct control, they would have the authority and credibility to force change on the international community.

This paper suggests a menu of strategic policies around

[I]n LDCs business-as-usual will not deliver the substantial acceleration necessary to keep pace … let alone catch up.

which LDC governments might rally. It focuses on new opportunities arising from recent changes in the world economy. It is easier to seize new opportunities than to revisit old battles. The most important opportunity will be the surge in extraction of natural resources from their territories; the scale of the financial flows will be without historic precedent for the LDCs. However, this will pose huge challenges of economic governance. This issue is discussed in Chapter 2. A further new challenge will be the consequences of the rise of the middle-income developing economies as industrial powers. Potentially, this makes it more difficult for the LDCs to diversify out of primary commodities into industrialisation. However, related developments in modern global manufacturing, notably trade-in-tasks, offer scope for new strategies. This is the subject of Chapter 3. LDCs have very small economies. Recent research suggests that very small scale is an impediment to development. The most realistic solution is regional integration, yet progress has been very slow. Revitalising regional integration is the subject of Chapter 4. The crisis in the OECD has worsened prospects for conventional development assistance, but opened prospects for more commercial forms of finance. This is the subject of Chapter 5. Finally, climate change and Asian growth are both posing new threats to food security in LDCs. This is the subject of Chapter 6.

2 The Challenge of Natural Resource Exploitation

Least developed countries have long been heavily dependent upon natural resource exports. This is both a problem and an opportunity. It is a problem because natural resource extraction does not directly employ many people and so has only limited direct transmission onto the incomes and well-being of ordinary citizens. Further, revenues are volatile, making macroeconomic management difficult and increasing the need for social protection.

It is, however, increasingly an opportunity. After decades of low prices for commodities, the growth of emerging market economies has driven up demand. For the foreseeable future commodity prices are likely to remain high. This will raise the resource revenues of LDCs twice over. Directly, high prices have the potential to raise revenues more than proportionately. This is because the taxable component of commodity export earnings is the rent – the excess of their value over the full costs of extraction. When commodity prices increase, costs do not rise proportionately, so the rent component increases more rapidly than the price. For example, when global commodity prices double, rents, and hence tax revenues, may triple.

In addition to this direct effect of high commodity prices on revenues, and probably more important, are the consequences for new discoveries. Until recently there has been much less prospecting in LDCs than in the richer countries. At the beginning of the twenty-first century, beneath a typical square mile of an LDC, the subsoil assets found were only one quarter of those found in a typical square mile of an OECD country (Collier, 2010). This is not because less is there, but because there has been less investment by resource extraction companies in searches in the LDCs.

For the foreseeable future commodity prices are likely to remain high. This will raise the resource revenues of LDCs twice over.

> *Primarily, the problems and opportunities call for distinctive domestic policies by LDC governments.*

Both the problems and the opportunities are peculiar to LDCs. Resource-rich OECD countries, such as Australia, Norway and Canada, have more diversified economies and are well-placed to cope with the problems posed by natural resources. Their opportunities for enhanced revenues are also more limited because they have less potential for new discoveries.

Primarily, the problems and opportunities call for distinctive domestic policies by LDC governments. However, some actions of the international community can also be helpful: these international actions are the focus of this paper.

Discovering and taxing natural resources

The discovery of natural resources is often an expensive, technically difficult and risky process. However, there are strong reasons for governments to commission the generation of good geological information which it can then make publicly available prior to selling prospecting rights. Without good prior public geological information two problems are likely: high private risks that heavily discount what prospectors are willing to pay; and 'asymmetric information', i.e. the prospectors will have much better information than the government as to what is likely to be found.

The costs of generating good public geological information are falling because of the development of aerial surveying techniques (such as those used recently by the Americans in Afghanistan). However, because for any one LDC government investment in geological information is risky, a better approach is to finance it through multilateral aid. If a multilateral donor uses aid for prospecting across many LDCs, the likelihood of finding valuable resources will be very high. This would probably be a high-return use of aid. Donors have been reluctant to use aid for this purpose because it is not 'photogenic' (i.e. does not yield direct social benefits), and perhaps because it weakens the bargaining power of international resource extraction companies. It is therefore an appropriate priority redeployment of aid for LDC governments to insist upon.

Once geological information has been generated, the challenge is to use this to maximise the amount of resource rents captured by the government. This depends upon the tax regime and initial payments in cash or kind. The best way for a government to maximise its bargaining power is to require competition between rival resource extraction companies or consortia: *competition between companies empowers LDC governments*. Companies prefer to deal with governments through secret, one-on-one negotiations or by offering packages which are not commensurable with other offers. This is the context which maximises their information advantage over governments. Companies can also use the structure of bilateral secret negotiations to play off one LDC government against another. LDC governments can realistically strengthen their joint bargaining power by insisting upon a common format for selling the rights to extraction, namely auctions conducted to common international standards, in which all bidders are competing in the same dimensions with the weights to be placed on each dimension made explicit (such as money and job commitments). Typically, a government gets a better deal if there are around four or five serious bidders. Fewer than this can result in collusion among bidders, while if there are too many bidders, no company is prepared to invest sufficiently in information to warrant a high bid – all companies bid low, knowing that one of them will be lucky. *Companies will be more willing to participate in such auctions if all LDCs require this approach than if only a few insist on it*. Hence, this is an area for common action. A good way of ensuring adherence by all LDCs to the auction approach is by setting it down as a voluntary international

The best way for a government to maximise its bargaining power is to require competition between rival resource extraction companies or consortia.

> *The more confidence that resource extraction firms have in the tax regime, the more will they be willing to invest in resource extraction.*

standard. That way, OECD governments can pressure their companies to engage on these terms.

While auctions are useful for maximising rent capture, the main instrument for rent capture is the tax regime. The more confidence that resource extraction firms have in the tax regime, the more likely they are to be willing to invest in resource extraction. This is because firms face an obvious 'time-consistency' problem. If the firm makes an irreversible investment based on a promise of low taxation, the government then has an incentive to break its commitment. As a sovereign power, the government has the authority to do this, but since the company recognises the risk, this power is a curse for the government rather than a blessing. For example, for decades the giant aluminium company ALCOA shipped bauxite out of Guinea rather than invest $1bn to build a smelter that would have reduced overall costs substantially. Its refusal to invest was explicitly because the government of Guinea lacked the power to make a *credible* commitment not to expropriate the investment through raising taxation. The inability to make credible commitments is not unique to LDC governments. (For example, after years of broken promises, most OECD governments have lost the power to make credible commitments on aid!) However, many LDC governments undoubtedly have this problem in respect of natural resource taxation. There are two complementary ways around this. First, a tax regime is more credible the more it builds in obvious contingencies, such as changes in world prices. Often tax regimes are changed because they have become highly disadvantageous to one party or another as a result of changes in circumstances that could have been anticipated. Designing such tax systems is complex because there is no single 'best practice'. The same commodity, such as copper, should be taxed differently, depending upon whether the country has high or low costs of extraction, and depending upon the expected lifetime of the deposits. Further, whether profits or gross revenues are the main object of taxation depends upon the capacity of the tax authorities to scrutinise what companies are reporting. Where there is limited capacity to scrutinise, it may be better to tax outcomes that are readily observable and difficult for companies to distort. Because the governments of LDCs do not have the capacity to design and run such tax systems and cannot afford to build it, they have a collective interest in the availability of free and independent international public expertise or equivalently in aid that can be used to purchase such expertise on the market. *The record of poorly designed tax regimes suggests that such assistance is not currently sufficiently available and so it is an appropriate demand on the international system from LDC governments.*

The other way around the problem is for LDC governments to use the international system to build ways of making their commitments credible. Currently, some LDC governments use the international Dispute Settlement Boards Mechanism: indeed China currently usually insists on such a clause in its contracts. An alternative, and perhaps better, approach would be to use the procedures of the WTO as an enforcement mechanism (Collier and Venables, 2010a). A core part of the WTO's purpose is to enforce government commitments, but to date this facility has seldom been used to help the governments of LDCs. This is paradoxical, since LDC governments have the greatest need of international commitment technologies. Of course, if resources are sufficiently valuable, some com-panies will be prepared to take the risks of investment, but even here companies implicitly recoup a hefty risk premium through the terms of the deal. *LDC governments can collectively help themselves by recognising that many of them have a credibility problem which is very costly to their own interests, and then using the international system to do something about it.*

LDC governments that favour such deals have a common interest in encouraging other countries to participate in auctions in which resources are sold in return for infrastructure.

Sometimes in LDCs the difficulties of ensuring efficient taxation and spending of revenues will be so daunting that governments may find it more advantageous to receive payment in kind. This is the approach commonly taken in deals with China: natural resources are sold in exchange for infrastructure. There are advantages to this approach, but it need not contravene the important principle that competition between bidders on clear and explicit dimensions will generate maximum benefits. Thus, if the government wants infrastructure, it can conduct an auction between bidders in terms of how much infrastructure each will provide. Although China is frequently criticised for the deals that it offers, the concern of LDC governments should be not that it offers a package approach of resources-for-infrastructure but that other countries do not, so that China is often a monopolist. Hence, *LDC governments that favour such deals have a common interest in encouraging other countries to participate in auctions in which resources are sold in return for infrastructure.*

Over time, countries can reasonably hope to build local expertise in the business of resource extraction, and also sometimes develop upstream and downstream industries. These objectives can therefore be legitimate requirements placed on resource extraction companies, although any such requirements are no stronger than the ability of government to monitor compliance. There is a danger that WTO rules may restrict the ability of governments to insist on local content procurement rules as an extension of general provisions to this effect. LDC governments should collectively resist such rules on the grounds that resource-rich, low-income countries face a distinctive need to diversify their economies. Local content procurement rules are not, therefore, simply a bias against international competition, but a possible strategy for an objective of diversification which is distinctive and appropriate.

Guarding against local violence and environmental damage

Both the Niger Delta and the Gulf of Mexico demonstrate the potential social and environmental risks involved in resource extraction. Clearly, these risks are greatest in LDCs. It is important to recognise that while resource extraction companies have an interest in managing these risks, their interest is not coincident with that of the government. Two sets of principles are likely to be important.

One is that the full costs of environmental damage should be borne by the company. This principle is important because only then does the company have a proper incentive to keep damage to a realistic minimum. Clearly, resource extraction companies do not have an interest in this principle. In the USA the judicial system provides this incentive, which is why the BP oil spill has been such a disaster for the company. But where judicial systems function less well, as in LDCs, companies are not credibly faced by the full costs. Remedying deficiencies in local legal systems can only happen in the long term. *In the meantime, there may be scope for establishing international and independent adjudication. The BP oil spill provides an ideal context in which LDC governments can get this issue on the global agenda.*

The other principle is that to the extent that is politically possible, the public revenues from resource extraction should accrue centrally to the government rather than to the locality where the resources are extracted. The centralisation of revenues permits their more equitable national distribution than if resource-rich localities are privileged. Again, resource extraction companies do not have an interest in this principle: generally, they would prefer public revenues to accrue to the locality in which they operate so as to minimise local opposition. However, the centralisation of revenues has historically often been associated with a heightened suspicion that

... the full costs of environmental damage should be borne by the company.

LDC governments ... have an interest in developing international mechanisms of transparency which build confidence in local populations that revenues are being well used.

they are being misappropriated, and as a consequence LDC governments face a credibility problem with the inhabitants of resource-rich localities. *LDC governments therefore have an interest in developing international mechanisms of transparency which build confidence in local populations that revenues are being well used.*

Guarding against corporate corruption

Governments are dependent upon individual officials and ministers to negotiate deals with resource extraction companies. Companies can gain immensely by bribing these individuals. This gives rise to an 'agency problem' for LDC governments. While widely recognised, to date it has been addressed by a variety of ad hoc international initiatives. One such is the Extractive Industries Transparency Initiative, started in 2003, which now has over 30 signatories among the governments of resource-rich countries, indicating recognition of concern for the problem. It aims to counter corruption in contracts by requiring companies engaged in resource extraction to report all their payments, country by country, forcing illicit payments into the open. Another initiative has been the pan-OECD anti-bribery legislation, which has made it a criminal offence for an OECD-based company to bribe government officials anywhere in the world in order to win a contract. One consequence of this OECD legislation has been the rapid emergence of a two-stage system of negotiations for the rights to resource extraction. In the first stage a company which is either too small to face scrutiny, or not OECD based, negotiates with government. In the second stage, this company sells on the rights to a major OECD company that has the technology and finance to undertake exploitation. A third and related international initiative has been to co-ordinate the laws relating to money laundering. A fourth initiative has been the Kimberley Process, which has curtailed illegal international transactions in diamonds through certification of the source of origin. The Government of Nigeria has recently proposed that an equivalent system of certification be put into place to curtail the large-scale theft of crude oil from the Nigerian delta. The latest initiative is the Lugar-Cardin Amendment, now enacted into US law, whereby all companies listed on the New York stock market engaged in resource extraction must report all payments made that are associated with contracts in considerable detail. Potentially, such legislation could so discourage the major companies from entering into prospecting contracts with the governments of LDCs that the only companies left as partners for governments would be cowboy operations.

Given the impediments to ad hoc international co-operative initiatives, this plethora of international responses is evidence of the need for a more systematic international approach. These initiatives could potentially be subsumed and made more effective by bringing corruption in resource extraction contracts under the clear remit of the WTO. For example, the anti-bribery legislation that the OECD now requires of its members could be a requirement of WTO membership, as could compliance with the equivalent of the Lugar-Cardin Amendment to the recent US Financial Reform Act. The emergence of major resource extraction companies based outside the OECD has made the WTO the appropriate institution for international co-operation on this matter. Countering corruption in international contracts faces an acute weakest link problem. So long as some companies are in jurisdictions where bribery is permitted, these companies will tend to win the contracts. Knowing this, individual governments that are the homes of resource extraction companies will be reluctant to act in isolation.

In principle, there is no reason why compliance by resource extraction companies with payments integrity could

LDC governments have a much stronger interest in countering corruption in resource contracts than OECD governments. International approaches… therefore depend upon LDC leadership.

not be built into WTO rules of membership. After all, the only conduct which is being discouraged is recognised as criminal in virtually all jurisdictions. Hence, it is not a matter of adopting new standards, but simply of enforcing standards which are already incorporated into legal systems globally. One major advantage is that this would throw the burden of enforcement back onto the governments that were the homes of resource extraction companies, rather than on the countries – often LDCs – in which they operate. A further advantage of using the WTO is that it is an organisation in which LDCs are represented, unlike the organisations which to date have been responsible for these initiatives, such as the OECD and the US Congress. *LDC governments have a much stronger interest in countering corruption in resource contracts than OECD governments. International approaches, while potentially effective, therefore depend upon LDC leadership.*

Saving and investing

Revenues from the extraction of natural resources are generated by depleting natural assets. This depletion should therefore be offset by the accumulation of other assets. While models of international best practice are often helpful, they must be appropriate. Currently, several LDC governments are following the practice of Norway and Kuwait, which have established funds for future generations. While this is sensible for Norway and Kuwait, it is inappropriate for LDCs. Both Norway and Kuwait have abundant invested capital per worker. In contrast, one of the defining features of LDCs is that they are short of capital. Hence, whereas it is appropriate for Norway and Kuwait to save their oil revenues in foreign financial assets, it is more sensible for LDCs to save by investing in their own country. Yet this inappropriate international 'best practice' has sometimes been foisted on LDCs. For example, the Chad–Cameroon pipeline project led to the creation of a future generations fund, which invested a proportion of the revenues from Chad's oil into foreign financial assets. Given the lack of public capital in Chad, this was unlikely to be the most appropriate use of these revenues.

Not only is the Norwegian-Kuwaiti model inappropriate for LDCs in terms of what assets are acquired, it is also inappropriate in terms of how much should be saved. A rich country that is depleting its natural assets should aim to save all the revenues and merely consume the income from these savings. In this way it uses resource depletion to increase its 'permanent income'. This approach is implicit in the standard IMF recommendation for how much to save out of resource revenues. However, for an LDC, the right objective is not to raise 'permanent income' but to speed up the process of convergence to global standards of consumption. In part this is achieved by using the revenues for investment, but resource revenues can also directly boost consumption towards global standards and this is a sensible use for an LDC. That these two uses of resource revenues are both legitimate in an LDC creates an inevitable tension between investment and consumption (Collier et al., 2009). Typically, the sensible range of saving out of resource revenues for an LDC will be 30–70 per cent – much higher than saving out of other forms of tax revenue, but substantially less than the 100 per cent implied by overly simple models of 'permanent income'. International models of 'best practice' such as that adopted by Norway are, however, highly influential. *The governments of LDCs have an interest in getting international recognition that the savings rates and asset choices appropriate for them are distinctive.*

Implications for managing 'Dutch disease'

The onset of resource exports can easily lead to 'Dutch disease', whereby the production of other internationally tradable goods (both exports and import substitutes)

The governments of LDCs have an interest in getting international recognition that the savings rates and asset choices appropriate for them are distinctive.

becomes uncompetitive. As a result, people employed in these activities can lose out, and the economy is undiversified and so dangerously exposed to commodity shocks. However, this is by no means inevitable. One conventional approach to avoiding Dutch disease has been to use much of the revenues to accumulate foreign financial assets, for example in sovereign wealth funds (SWFs). However, as discussed above, as a continuous strategy this is largely inappropriate for an LDC: the country should be accumulating assets domestically, rather than abroad. The accumulation of foreign assets can nevertheless be important during commodity price booms to prevent spikes in the exchange rate which could bankrupt non-resource exporters. Whether this spending on domestic investment gives rise to Dutch disease depends upon how, specifically, it is used. Typically, the non-resource export sector of LDCs faces high costs due to inadequate infrastructure for transport and power. By investing in these sectors the government can fully avoid Dutch disease: an appreciation in the real exchange rate is offset by the reductions in cost. More ambitiously, domestic investment can pump-prime new export activities. That Dutch disease is not inevitable is illustrated by the contrast between Nigeria and Indonesia following their oil discoveries. The Nigerian cocoa industry went into severe decline, but over the same period Indonesia developed a cocoa industry and rapidly became a major exporter (Bevan *et al.*, 1999).

Synthesising the issues

Over the next decade the extraction of natural resources from LDCs is likely to expand both in value and volume. It is a unique opportunity for LDCs, but the history of resource extraction is not encouraging: harnessing the opportunity requires a capacity to resist pressures of both corruption and populism. Neither the interests of the OECD countries nor those of the emerging market economies are the same as the interests of the LDCs. Nor are the available models of OECD 'best practice' particularly appropriate for LDCs.

There is thus a strong case for LDC governments to adopt voluntary norms that are pertinent for developing countries and independent of interest groups. Until recently no such norms were available. Now, however, there are two complementary voluntary international standards, the Extractive Industries Transparency Initiative (EITI), and the Natural Resource Charter. The EITI is a multi-stakeholder international organisation that focuses exclusively on the transparency of revenues. Currently around 30 governments are using it as a commitment technology and as a mutual commitment device for governments and companies. LDCs should find it useful. The Natural Resource Charter is an information guide on the decisions involved in harnessing natural resources for development. It is managed by an independent oversight board with members from Africa, Asia, Latin America and the Middle East, and is chaired by Ernesto Zedillo (ex-President of Mexico). The Board is supported by a technical group headed by economics Nobel Laureate Michael Spence. It sets out the entire decision chain involved in harnessing natural resources for development on a website (www.natural resourcecharter.org) intended for governments, citizens and companies. Its 12 precepts propose standards for resource extraction companies, the governments which are the home of such companies and the governments of the countries in which resources are being extracted. The Charter has been endorsed by the African Development Bank. While not designed for commitments, it is appropriate for LDCs. *Their governments may find endorsement of it useful to indicate in general terms the policies and standards they expect to follow.*

Their governments may find endorsement of [the Natural Resource Charter] useful to indicate in general terms the policies and standards they expect to follow.

17

3 Using Trade Preferences to Help LDCs Break into Global Manufacturing

Trade preferences for LDCs continue to be part of the world trading system. Under the Generalised System of Preferences (GSP), LDCs have access to most OECD markets and historical ties have been recognised in schemes such as the European Union's Lomé and Cotonou agreements. Recent years have seen several major extensions of preference schemes. The EU's Everything but Arms scheme, initiated in 2001, gave duty free access to LDCs in almost all products. The USA introduced the African Growth and Opportunities Act (AGOA) in 2000, improving market access for eligible sub-Saharan African countries. The USA also operates the Caribbean Basin Initiative (CBI) and the Andean Trade Promotion Act.[1]

These schemes have two main elements. One is the trade preference – the granting of market access at reduced tariff rates and with less restrictive quotas, possibly going all the way to duty and quota free market access. The other is constraints on participation. These define eligible countries and products, and also impose rules of origin (ROOs). There has frequently been a tension between these elements, with the constraints severely reducing the effectiveness of preferences as an instrument of economic development. These constraints are likely to be particularly important for manufactured products and redesign of preferences is needed if they are to facilitate developing country participation in a globalised world trading system.

The benefits of trade preferences accrue through two mechanisms. The one usually emphasised is a transfer of rent to recipient (developing) countries. Instead of being received

... redesign of preferences is needed if they are to facilitate developing country participation in a globalised world trading system.

... employment in manufacturing exports can be expanded without running into diminishing returns to scale due to markets or endowments.

by the developed country importer as tariff revenue or quota rent, the preference margin is instead transferred to producers in exporting countries. The magnitude of the rent transfer has been calculated by various researchers. A recent study estimates an upper bound (preference margins x the value of trade) of only US$500m accruing to LDCs.[2] This is too small to be worth serious policy attention.

However, preferences can also generate benefits through a second mechanism: there may be a significant export supply response, creating employment in developing countries. This is the focus of the present paper. While the rent transfer mechanism depends upon the existing quantity of exports, the supply response mechanism depends upon the potential of unrealised opportunities. For many LDCs this distinction between actual and potential exports approximates to that between agriculture and manufactures. For most LDCs, their current rents from trade preferences depend upon market access for their existing agricultural exports, whereas preferences in manufactures might enable them to break into markets that they have scarcely entered. Of course, rents for agricultural exports will also generate some quantity effect. However, the potential magnitude of the quantity effect is far greater in manufacturing exports.

One reason for the greater potential is liberation from diminishing returns to scale. Production of manufactures for the domestic market encounters diminishing returns due to the constraint of small market size. Traditional agricultural and resource-based exports encounter diminishing returns because of limited endowments of suitable land and hence declining resource base per worker. By contrast, employment in manufacturing exports can be expanded without running into diminishing returns to scale due to markets or endowments. The other reason for the greater potential is that manufacturing exports are subject to scale thresholds which can generate multiple stable equilibria. The scale thresholds arise because of well-documented external economies that advantage those firms that are located within a cluster of similar firms. Potentially viable export locations may be uncompetitive relative to established clusters and so never develop unless induced. Hence, not only may trade preferences in manufactures generate a large supply response, they may switch a location to a new equilibrium and so have permanent effects even if they are only implemented temporarily.[3]

The importance of manufacturing and other modern sector exports to the wider process of economic growth is now supported by a good deal of evidence. The Asian experience is well documented, and a number of recent studies point to the role of exports in growth accelerations (Hausmann *et al.*, 2005). Jones and Olken (2006) identify growth accelerations, and show that these are associated with an average 13 percentage point increase in the share of trade in income (over a five-year period), as well as an acceleration of the rate of transfer of labour into manufacturing. Pattillo *et al.* (2005) point to the association between growth accelerations and trade growth in sub-Saharan Africa.

How can trade preferences be designed to maximise their effectiveness in stimulating a manufacturing supply response? Manufacturing supply response is not a simple matter of moving up a supply curve, but depends on a wide range of complementary inputs, some of which can be imported and some of which must be developed domestically, often involving increasing returns to scale. Trade preferences can have a catalytic role, but only if they are designed to allow the import of complementary inputs, and to operate in countries with the skills and infrastructure to be near the threshold of global manufacturing competitiveness.

Trade preferences can have a catalytic role … if they are designed to allow the import of complementary inputs …

Tightly restrictive ROOs leave countries unable to use preferences to exploit a comparative advantage in a narrowly defined task ...

How modern manufacturing works

Modern sector production is not simply a matter of transforming primary factors into final output. It requires primary factors and many other complementary inputs, ranging from specialist skills and knowledge to component parts. These are frequently supplied by many different countries, with design, engineering, marketing and component production occurring in different places – a process known as fragmentation of production. Furthermore, productivity levels in these different activities are not exogenously fixed. They are shaped by learning and by complementarities with other activities.

Modern global manufacturing production is 'fragmenting' – a process known as unbundling or splitting the value chain (UNIDO, 2009). Different stages involved in producing a particular final good are now often performed in many different countries. Particular tasks may be outsourced (or offshored) and can be undertaken in different places. This occurs in response to productivity or factor price differences and may take place within a single multinational firm or through production networks of supplier firms. Fragmentation implies that comparative advantage now resides in quite narrowly defined tasks. For some products tasks may be undertaken in parallel and then assembled in a single place. For others a sequential production process still applies, under which each task adds value to a product that crosses borders at each stage. In this case, the partially completed product is an essential input to the task to be performed at the next stage. The effect of tightly restrictive ROOs is to prohibit participation in production processes of this type. Tightly restrictive ROOs leave countries unable to use preferences to exploit a comparative advantage in a narrowly defined task; instead they have to undertake a wide range of tasks domestically to meet ROO requirements, but this wide range of locally performed tasks, some of which are liable to be more costly than the world standard, then makes the activity globally uncompetitive.

The fragmentation of global manufacturing is good news for LDCs because it enables them to break in one task at a time. However, the other major trend, clustering, is bad news. Clustering arises because increasing returns to scale are often external to the individual firm, meaning that firms in a particular location gain from the presence of other firms in related activities. One set of mechanisms creating these external returns to scale is technological externalities arising as firms learn from other firms, observing and borrowing best practice technique. The knowledge discovered need not be sophisticated technology: it might simply be discovery of the fact that it is possible to undertake a particular type of business profitably in a particular location. This has a demonstration effect which underlies theories of social learning and which Hausmann and Rodrik (2003) have termed 'economic development as self-discovery'.

In addition to technological externalities, there are a number of pecuniary externalities associated with provision of complementary inputs. As a cluster of firms grows, so specialist input suppliers develop, markets for intermediate goods become thicker, transport and infrastructure support improves and workers have a greater incentive to acquire skills.[4] For example, consider a downstream industry that requires specialist inputs from upstream firms, or specialist skills from its workers. If there is only one firm in the downstream industry there will be no incentive for upstream suppliers or workers to invest in improving quality or acquiring skills, since they will be 'held up' by the monopsony power of the downstream firm. Only once the downstream industry is large enough is there an incentive for its suppliers to upgrade and thereby raise the productivity of the combined operation. Research on cities suggests that, over a wide range

The fragmentation of global manufacturing is good news for LDCs because it enables them to break in one task at a time.

... over a wide range of city sizes, each doubling of size raises productivity by between 3 and 8 per cent.

of city sizes, each doubling of size raises productivity by between 3 and 8 per cent. The effects often operate over quite a small spatial range – within a city or travel-to-work area. The benefits may be shared among a number of sectors (as with improved transport or more regular shipping services), but are often quite sector or task specific.

An important consequence of spatially concentrated increasing returns is that comparative advantage is, in part, *acquired* rather than fundamental. A particular location may have no inherent advantage in a sector or task, but as a cluster starts to develop, so costs fall, creating the comparative advantage.

Implications for LDC governments

Fragmentation and clustering imply that modern sector export growth is likely to be uneven. Activity may be concentrated in small spatial areas – cities will acquire particular specialisations. There will be threshold effects; establishing a new activity in the face of existing competition may be quite difficult, but once it gets established costs start to fall and growth can become extremely rapid.[5] An extreme example of product and spatial concentration is the city of Qiaotou, producing 60 per cent of the world's buttons. As for threshold effects, Bangladesh shipped its first consignment of garments to the USA in 1978, had exports of US$600 million by 1990 and more than US$6 billion by 2005, employing 2.5 million people.

What are the implications of these facts for LDCs wanting to break into manufacturing but having low levels of both hard and soft infrastructure, such as countries in sub-Saharan Africa? Successful participation in production networks and fragmented production processes requires a business environment that delivers security, contract enforcement and protection from predation. It also requires a level of infrastructure that can support continuous production and reliable delivery. However, the fact of spatial concentration means that it is not necessary that high quality infrastructure is provided everywhere – it can be provided in selected areas or in special economic zones. This is positive for those LDCs that hope to break into manufacturing, since it economises on these scarce inputs. Infrastructure (and institutions) can be targeted so that some areas work well, and this is more efficient than spreading infrastructure at a uniformly low level.

That modern global manufacturing enables countries to specialise on a narrow product or task range is also positive for new entrants. Instead of having to learn and acquire comparative advantage in all stages of a product's production, fragmentation makes it possible to progress incrementally, first learning narrow tasks, such as production of a particular type of garment using imported textiles and yarn. However, barriers to trade in intermediate goods are a critical obstacle to this. The barriers may arise because of domestic import restrictions, because of high trade costs due to geography and infrastructure, or because of rules of origin. They all have the effect of inhibiting participation in global production networks.

Co-ordination failures imply that getting started is hard: it is only once a threshold has been passed that increasing returns start to reduce costs. This calls for some sort of catalytic action to overcome initial obstacles and get to the threshold level. This in turn has implications for trade and industrial policy in general and trade preferences in particular.

Past discussion of industrialisation strategies for new entrant LDCs has generally focused upon the trade policies of their own governments. Changes in their trade policies are indeed a necessary part of catalytic action, but not in the form most commonly envisaged. For an LDC-based firm to succeed in exporting a new manufacturing 'task', it would

That modern global manufacturing enables countries to specialise on a narrow product or task range is ... positive for new entrants.

Africa's ... locations are not currently identical to those of Asia – they have higher costs due to the lack of clusters.

need to be able to import without restriction all the complementary upstream tasks. Hence, the catalytic trade policy for LDC governments is to remove their current tariffs on manufactured inputs. For example, in West Africa the Economic Community of West African States (ECOWAS) imposes a uniform 10 per cent tariff on all such inputs. While 10 per cent may appear modest, suppose that in the absence of trade impediments an Africa-based firm chooses to import inputs constituting half of the value of its output, so that the tariff raises its total costs by 5 per cent. Now consider what this implies for what the firm can afford to pay as labour costs. Even in labour-intensive manufacturing, labour costs typically only constitute around 16 per cent of total cost. Hence, to keep its total costs constant in the face of the tariff on inputs, the firm would need an offsetting reduction in its labour costs to 11 per cent. Thus, to compete with firms based in a location that was identical, other than that it did not impose tariffs on inputs, the firm would need to pay wages that were around one third lower. Of course, Africa's problem arises precisely because its locations are *not* currently identical to those of Asia – they have higher costs due to the lack of clusters. Tariffs on inputs intensify the problem rather than resolve it.

Should an astute government adopt a tariff structure with zero tariffs on inputs but positive tariffs on final goods? There are several reasons why such a strategy would also fail. First, the country's niche in the long chain of manufacturing 'tasks' that eventually generate a final product is unlikely to be precisely the final 'task'. For any task prior to this the protection would be useless. And products which are 'final' to one industry are 'inputs' to another. As the above examples demonstrate, modern manufacturing niches are so specialised that the domestic market for them in the typical LDC is too small to be a significant inducement to relocation. How important is the prospect of a price premium in the Tanzanian market for buttons in determining whether firms selling on the global market should relocate their production from Qiaotou? Even in the unlikely event that such protection would be significant, the political difficulties for the Tanzanian government of imposing high tariffs on buttons alongside free trade in all the myriad inputs that button producers want to use would surely be overwhelming.

An alternative style of industrial policy for an LDC government would be to subsidise the costs of production rather than protect the domestic market. But such policies have a poor track record. As a claim on government expenditure it would have to compete with manifestly pressing social needs. Further, the most conventional form of subsidy, tax incentives for investment, subsidises capital and this can be at the expense of employment. Untargeted production subsidies would be expensive because existing production for the domestic market would qualify, but targeting requires information that is typically not available to government, and a degree of discretion that risks eliding into corruption.[6] Perhaps the most effective way of targeting a subsidy towards exporting firms is to provide good quality infrastructure for geographically-defined export zones, but since Asian governments already do this, it may be merely a necessary, but not sufficient, condition for inducing relocation.

Unlike these forms of industrial policy, trade preferences in OECD markets are not under the control of LDC governments; like aid, they are an instrument of development policies under the control of OECD governments. However, they have some major advantages over the policies that are available to LDC governments to provide the (temporary) advantage needed to get cluster formation. First, they are relatively immune from recipient country political economy problems, since they are set by foreign, not domestic, govern-

[trade preferences] have some major advantages over the policies that are available to LDC governments to provide the ... advantage needed to get cluster formation.

> *Mauritius is the only African country to have decisively penetrated global markets in manufacturing.*

ments. Thus, there is no way in which their level can be escalated in support of failing firms. Second, since trade preferences support exports, they offer a performance-based incentive – firms benefit only if they export. Firms therefore face the discipline – on quality as well as on price – imposed by international competition. Rodrik (2004) argues that this discipline has been an important positive factor underlying the success of export-oriented strategies, as compared to import substitution. Finally, they are fiscally costless to LDC governments and virtually costless to OECD governments and so do not compete with government spending on social needs or with aid.

Is there any evidence that trade preferences have had a positive effect on modern sector production? Before answering this question we need to be clear about what effects we expect. Preferences will be valuable if countries are able to participate in fragmentation and production networks. This is facilitated by liberal ROOs and by geographical proximity, as well as by standard determinants of comparative advantage. Even if these circumstances are met, their effects might be concentrated in a few sectors, regions or countries, and only set in above some threshold.

Mauritius is the only African country to have decisively penetrated global markets in manufacturing, in the process transforming itself from an impoverished sugar island to Africa's highest-income economy. Famously, this performance defied the forecast of Nobel Laureate James Meade that the country was condemned to poverty. Subramanian and Roy (2003) investigate the reasons for the take-off. They find that export manufacturing success was the foremost proximate reason for economic success. In turn, the success in manufacturing was triggered by two coincident strategies. The Mauritian government granted duty free inputs for manufactured exports; Subramanian and Roy find this to have been quantitatively important. However, they find that the OECD decision to grant Mauritius trade preferences in garments through the multi-fibre agreement (MFA) was even more important. Crucially, the MFA gave Mauritius privileged access to OECD markets relative to established Asian producers. The MFA ended in 2004, but Mauritius is now well-established in OECD markets and has gradually shifted to more complex manufacturing 'tasks'. The temporary preference scheme was thus critical in permanently transforming the Mauritian economy.

The African Growth and Opportunities Act, which gives trade preferences to African countries in the US market, offers duty free access for a wide range of products. AGOA is not restricted to LDCs, and is currently available to 38 African countries, including Kenya, Nigeria and South Africa.[7] AGOA ROOs are strict (varying across products, but generally with inputs having to come from the USA or other AGOA countries). However, they were relaxed for apparel under the 'special rule' clause. This allows eligible countries to use fabric imported from third countries in their apparel exports to the USA so that the ROO is just a 'single transformation requirement' (i.e. the transformation from fabric to garment must be undertaken in the eligible country). This special rule is temporary and has been renewed under a series of waivers. The special rule now applies to 25 African countries (including Kenya and Nigeria, but not South Africa). Study of the effects of AGOA is particularly informative, as it can be compared with the EU's trade preferences under the Cotonou agreement and EBA. These are in many respects similar, but (a) have more restrictive ROOs for apparel, and (b) have a somewhat different country coverage, with only LDCs being eligible. Collier and Venables (2007) show that AGOA has been highly successful in expanding African apparel exports to the USA, whereas EBA has failed

... AGOA has been highly successful in expanding African apparel exports to the USA, whereas EBA has failed to do the same for African exports to the EU.

> *... trade preferences, even if temporary, can be effective in helping new entrants to break into global manufacturing.*

to do the same for African exports to the EU. They attribute this predominantly to the more liberal ROOs for apparel provided by the 'special rule' of AGOA than are available under EBA. In other words, trade preferences, even if temporary, can be effective in helping new entrants to break into global manufacturing. However, they need to be combined with generous ROOs and limited to countries that have not already broken into global markets.

For Africa and other currently unindustrialised LDCs to diversify their exports into manufacturing may require a catalyst to create clusters of activity and lift them to threshold productivity levels. Forty years of African domestic protectionism has failed to induce such clusters. However, the evidence suggests that – given the right conditions – it is possible for African countries to accelerate their modern sector export growth. Designing policy to promote such growth requires recognition of a number of features of modern global trade: fragmentation, increasing returns and the consequent lumpiness of development. Domestic policy and international policy complement each other. Domestic policy needs to ensure a good business environment and infrastructure, but this can be spatially concentrated. International policy needs to redesign trading arrangements with ROOs that do not penalise narrow specialisation. Two of the past initiatives in trade preferences for African manufactures, the MFA and AGOA, have both demonstrated their effectiveness. However, at the time when the MFA was launched, few African governments had adopted the complementary policies needed for success, and the MFA has now ended. The key feature that made AGOA effective, the apparel special waiver, has now been renewed, but AGOA applies only to the US market and to selected African countries.

The experience of trade preferences has demonstrated that as devices for transferring income ('rents') to LDCs they are largely ineffective. For this purpose they are simply not worth prioritising as an objective. However, the experience has also demonstrated that as devices for pump-priming the entry of a country into global manufacturing, in particular the manufacture of apparel, they can be useful. For them to work three conditions need to be in place.

First, the rules of origin need to be sufficiently generous that LDC specialisation in one or two tasks in the production of a product is eligible. However, ROO should not be so generous that the only activity that takes place in the LDC is relabelling of products manufactured elsewhere. The AGOA rules of origin appear to be about right.

Second, the governments of LDCs need to complement privileged market access by encouraging the formation of a cluster of firms in an export processing zone (EPZ). Although EPZs have been the standard approach for breaking into manufacturing used in Asia, in several LDCs they have a very mixed record. An EPZ is only likely to work if it provides an efficient location for production: an EPZ which is badly located and inadequately serviced cannot be made to work just by granting tax concessions. Tax concessions are much less important that genuine reductions in the costs of production. The most effective form of inducement is to select a good location at a well-functioning port. Firms should then be clustered in this location: attempts to spread manufacturing thinly around the country on considerations of equity are likely to be doomed to failure. Once a good port location has been selected, costs of production can be reduced through the provision of adequate physical infrastructure and efficient administration of services such as customs and regulation. To increase the confidence of firms in this provision it may be helpful to commit to certain standards of service, such as the maximum time taken for customs clearance. The necessary infrastructure may well be a good use of aid, and this would

... attempts to spread manufacturing thinly around the country on considerations of equity are likely to be doomed to failure.

encourage practical policy coherence on the part of OECD governments – their trade policies would be aligned with their aid policies.

Third, unfortunately, privileged market access can only work to pump-prime new entrants to manufacturing if all established producers are excluded. As in the UNIDO proposal of 2009, the remit of the scheme has to be confined to least-developed-in-manufacturing countries (UNIDO, 2009). This is because if even one established producer is included in the scheme, their initial cost advantage from having an already formed cluster of producers will make new entrants uncompetitive: international firms will take advantage of the privileged access by expanding production in the established cluster. While most established manufacturing clusters are in emerging market economies, a few are in LDCs, such as the apparel cluster in Bangladesh. Unfortunately, it is essential that such producers not be included in the coverage of the scheme.

Subject to these three conditions the appropriate market for privileged access is as near to being global as is politically possible. *The minimum reasonable political goal for privileged market access is for all least-developed-in-manufacturing countries to be included in a common, OECD-wide scheme.* A common scheme would be more effective than piecemeal different schemes with individual OECD countries: it would be easier for firms to understand and use, and politically more robust. Since the objective is to pump-prime the formation of clusters, it is not necessary for the scheme to be permanent. A temporary scheme might be easier to negotiate, being more acceptable both to the USA and to countries not covered (such as Bangladesh), and less liable to opposition in the WTO (where AGOA already has a waiver). A common OECD-wide scheme would involve harmonising the American scheme AGOA, with the EU schemes, EBA and economic partnership agreements (EPAs). This is a timely moment to request the EU to rethink its trade preferences: the European trade schemes are manifestly in a degree of disarray and there is a new European Commission that is not necessarily so committed to past arrangements.

While a common OECD scheme is a reasonable minimum negotiating objective, ideally it should include *preferential access to the emerging market economies (EMEs)*. Collectively, the EMEs are now a large and fast-growing market and so it would be advantageous for LDCs to gain access to them. Politically, it is important to accelerate the process whereby EMEs reconceptualise themselves from being fellow victims alongside LDCs of an international system in which they are powerless to recognise their new status as significant players who should share the responsibility for assisting LDCs. For the EMEs, the most appropriate form of assistance for LDCs is their trade policies. Their markets are far more protected from LDC products than those of the OECD, while liberalising them selectively towards LDCs would not involve significant fiscal costs.

A common, OECD-wide privileged market access scheme for those developing countries yet to break into manufacturing was initially proposed in Collier and Venables (2007). It has recently been endorsed by François Bourguignon (former Chief Economist of the World Bank) and by Nancy Birdsall (President of the Center for Global Development).

... a common OECD scheme ... should include preferential access to the emerging market economies.

4 Regional Integration

Most LDCs remain predominantly rural. All have small economies, and most also have small populations. As the above discussion of industrialisation indicates, modern economies are characterised by scale economies which accrue in cities. Such scale economies are not confined to manufacturing: they also apply to the many service activities which in a modern economy employ most people. Countries that are small and predominantly rural are not well placed to reap such scale economies. Their populations are spatially dispersed and their national markets are too small. The costs of being small are partly that urban scale economies cannot be achieved, and partly that markets are too thin and therefore uncompetitive.

To overcome this problem there is a strong case for regional integration. By integrating markets regionally the size of the market is increased. Markets support a larger hierarchy of cities and also become more competitive.

However, despite these powerful benefits, to date regional integration among developing countries has been painfully slow: there has been plenty of lip-service and a multitude of integration schemes, but on the ground trade barriers have remained in place. Part of the explanation for this failure is that integration has been regarded as a strategy for industrialisation: a protected regional market would enable manufacturing to get established. This is the wrong rationale for regional integration.

Regional integration does not deliver industrialisation. It focuses on the wrong market: manufacturing is now a global activity, and the key markets for LDC manufactures are not LDCs themselves but the OECD and potentially the EMEs. As discussed in the previous chapter, barriers to imports, whether nationally or regionally administered, impede entry into global manufacturing because they raise the cost of

… there is a strong case for regional integration. By integrating markets regionally the size of the market is increased.

> *Productivity tends to be higher in large (and/or dense) clusters of economic activity. This is the reason why cities form.*

imported inputs into production. Further, regionally focused industrialisation has proved to be politically divisive. Typically, industry has concentrated in the more developed countries of a common regional market, selling its production at prices above world levels to the LDC countries in the region. Naturally, LDC governments have been reluctant to take part in such arrangements.

The true case for regional integration is not primarily about manufacturing, but about urbanisation and market size.

Regional integration, urbanisation and productivity

Productivity tends to be higher in large (and/or dense) clusters of economic activity. This is the reason why cities form. Firms and workers locate to gain the benefits of this productivity advantage, despite the congestion costs and other diseconomies associated with large cities. A number of mechanisms drive this productivity effect. Some are narrowly technical, for example the fact that dense activity economises on transport costs, and improves communications and learning. Firms are better able to connect with each other and workers are better able to connect with firms. Other mechanisms are to do with the impact of size on market structure, something discussed further below. Still others are to do with political economy: a city with a large business sector is likely to have a strong business lobby and so a business-friendly investment climate. The quantitative evidence of the productivity effect of city size comes largely from studies of cities in developed countries. The consensus view is that doubling city size is associated with a productivity increase of around 6 per cent. This is a large effect – moving from a city of 100,000 workers to one of 3 million is predicted to increase productivity by more than 30 per cent.

There are few studies for developing countries. One for Chinese cities finds even larger effects: moving from a city of 100,000 workers to one of 1.3 million workers raises productivity by 80 per cent. However, tentative evidence for LDCs suggests that there the normal global relationship whereby larger city size raises productivity may not be occurring. Bringing people together in cities has two potentially offsetting effects. People bring income and skills, which increase market size, but they also place demands on living space which increases congestion. In most parts of the globe the former effect appears to dominate, so that the larger is the city the higher is productivity. But in LDCs the gains to market size may be fully offset by the additional costs of congestion. The degree of congestion generated by population growth depends upon urban planning and infrastructure investment. A likely implication is that LDCs have not paid sufficient attention to these policies for managing congestion. As a result, the large potential gains in productivity from city growth (as experienced in China), have not been realised. Not only are cities too small, but they are unproductive because of unmanaged congestion. Managing congestion, and especially acting in anticipation of urban growth, are likely to be good uses of public resources, both aid and domestic revenues. The persistent donor emphasis upon rurally directed social agendas has perhaps discouraged governments from providing the urban infrastructure that in other countries is deployed to offset congestion. Governments need to make this case more strongly with donors.

The political fragmentation of LDCs into small economies has repercussions for city size. Cities tend to be much smaller than in an integrated polity such as India. Collier and Venables (2010b) find that a merger of two similar size small countries, thereby doubling both population and area, would lead to a 75 per cent increase in the size of the largest city. To see the quantitative implications of this, suppose that initially there are ten separate small coun-

> *Small economies are likely to have high levels of monopoly power. This reduces their attractiveness for new investment.*

tries, in each of which the largest city has a population of 3 million people. Combining these countries and letting city sizes adjust in line with the regularities found globally has dramatic effects on city size. In the newly integrated region, one of the cities that initially had only 3 million people would grow to become a mega-city of 19 million. Another would grow to 9.5 million and a third to 6.3 million. This massive growth would overwhelmingly come from a shift of population from rural to urban locations rather than from other cities. Six of the ten cities would grow overall as a result of regional integration, their combined populations rising from 18 million to 46 million. Of the increase in this urbanised population of 28 million, 90 per cent would come from a shift from rural areas. The other four cities would shrink a little, from a combined population of 12 million to 9.1 million.

This analysis suggests that the smaller size of LDC cities compared to those in other developing countries is due, in large part, to the fragmentation of countries. Our preceding analysis and the evidence from developed country studies implies that this has an adverse effect on productivity.

Regional integration, market size and competition

Small economies are likely to have high levels of monopoly power. This reduces their attractiveness for new investment. Directly, the price effects associated with monopoly make investment goods expensive. Less directly, the lack of innovation associated with incumbent monopoly reduces the pressure to invest. Least obvious, but perhaps most important, monopoly creates the potential for opportunistic behaviour in transactions.

Evidently, a small market is likely to be less competitive than a large one as, given some firm-level economies of scale, fewer firms will operate. The effect will be particularly pronounced in sectors closed to trade. For example, the typical LDC economy has a very highly concentrated banking sector: often four banks dominate lending and this is a small enough number to enable collusive oligopoly. The limited nature of the market also leads to a concentration of risks: banks are exposed to a high covariance of the risk of default.

Transport is another sector that is sheltered from international competition and that is often highly cartelised. A recent study of transport in Africa finds that trucking firms are able to charge exceptionally high prices even though their real costs are not abnormally high (Teravaninthorn and Raballand, 2008). Average prices per ton kilometre are US$0.02 in Pakistan, US$0.05 in China, US$0.08 for the Mombasa-Kampala run and US$0.11 for Doula-N'Djamena. Many LDCs have restrictive regulatory regimes and transport cartels. Breaking these can have a big pay-off. For example, in Rwanda the deregulation of the trucking industry reduced transport prices by an estimated 75 per cent. For some countries, a major factor supporting cartelisation is a treaty structure between countries designed to protect the national trucking industry from competition from neighbouring countries.

Monopoly power raises prices. A key price is that of capital goods. The higher the price of capital goods, the less physical equipment an expenditure on investment will purchase. This effect is big, as the price of capital goods can be three or four times higher in LDCs than it is in high-income countries. Why is there this price difference? In part it is due to thin markets and monopoly power in supply of equipment and investment goods. Because LDCs have low per capita incomes, small populations and low investment rates, their national markets for capital goods are much smaller than those of other countries. Collier and Venables (2010b) show that both small population and low per capita income substantially raise the price of capital goods.

... both small population and low per capita income substantially raise the price of capital goods.

Thin markets and the resulting monopoly power thus increase the price of capital goods. They have further pernicious effects. One is that they create an incentive for incumbent firms to actively pursue strategies that deter the entry of new firms. From the perspective of firms that are already operating in a sector, if one firm devotes resources to keeping new entrants out of the sector, this is a public good. The strategies of entry deterrence may be the use of predatory pricing or the purchase of political influence. Evidently, from the perspective of society as a whole such behaviour is undesirable. In an industry with many existing firms the free-riding problem implies that the returns to any one firm from such anti-social behaviour are limited. But in a small market with an incumbent monopolist all the benefits to the existing industry are internalised and so the incentive to act to keep out new competitors is maximised.

Small and thin markets are also unattractive places to invest because investors are vulnerable to 'hold-up' – opportunistic behaviour by other firms with which they have to transact. Hold-up refers to the possibility that, once an investment has been sunk, the investor faces a monopsonistic purchaser of the output of the investment. Even if the purchaser and investor entered an agreement before the investment is undertaken, *ex post* the purchaser may act opportunistically, breaking the agreement and only offering a lower price. The investor will anticipate this possibility of hold-up, so may not make the investment in the first place. The only realistic way of overcoming the hold-up problem is to make sure that there are many alternative uses for the output of the project. In turn this depends upon the size of the market in which the output is sold. Hold-up is more likely the fewer people are competing for the output. This suggests that in small economies the threat of hold-up may be a major deterrent to investment. In agriculture, returns to investment are reduced if there is a monopsonistic grain merchant. In manufacturing, if there are only a few potential purchasers of output it will deter investment. This gives rise to co-ordination failure – there is no incentive to enter on one side of the market until the other side has got more firms, and vice versa. And, in a small economy, even the return to the worst option, liquidating the investment, may be reduced by thin markets for second-hand capital equipment. Distress sales are likely to be more coincident because smaller economies are less diversified, further depressing the expected price. The hold-up phenomenon applies not only to goods markets, but also to labour markets; the incentive to take training is reduced if the skill acquired can only be sold to one employer.

These arguments point to the fact that smallness does not just create static monopoly/monopsony power, but also creates a fundamentally more risky business environment. Entry of new producers will be deterred by the predatory behaviour of incumbents and by the scarcity of outside options and consequent vulnerability to predatory and opportunistic behaviour.

Implications for LDCs

Both the gains from urbanisation and those from more competitive markets imply that LDCs need regional integration far more than other economies. Yet to date they have made less progress than others. The damaging effects of regional integration on the poorest member countries come not from integration *per se*, but from protection of the regional market from global competition. *For LDCs the gains from regional integration come not from protection from global markets, but from the expansion beyond tiny national markets.* This suggests that within regional integration schemes LDCs should lobby for low external protection: high regional protection will

For LDCs the gains from regional integration come not from protection from global markets, but from the expansion beyond tiny national markets.

redistribute income from LDCs to more developed member countries. Further, many of the gains for LDCs from integration will come from creating regional markets in services such as trucking, where protection from the global market is irrelevant.

The above should not be mistaken for an unqualified appeal for trade liberalisation. As discussed above, in order to break into global markets for manufactures, LDCs need protection *in those markets* from established producers. Firms producing in LDCs for these external markets also need supporting infrastructure and regulatory policies that are comparable to those of established competitors. But it does point to a need to rethink the traditional approach to protected regional markets.

5 Innovations in Financing Development

Until recently, the only financing for government permitted to LDCs was official development assistance. The prospects for aggregate ODA are not encouraging: unprecedented fiscal pressures in OECD countries are reducing aid budgets. There is a need both to sharpen the focus of ODA onto LDCs, and to look to alternatives.

Sharpening the focus of ODA on LDCs

Given that the prospects for total aid are discouraging, a sensible strategy for the governments of LDCs is to focus attention on its allocation. While the ostensible rationale for aid is to address poverty, most aid goes to countries that are not LDCs. Indeed, large aid flows are going to middle-income countries that are already growing rapidly. If aid were focused on LDCs it would permit a major expansion in the aid flow to LDCs without requiring any increase in OECD aid budgets. As the category of emerging market economy expands, it is important that these countries cease to be aid recipients so that aid can be concentrated on those countries that really need it. In making the case for reallocating aid, three rationales for providing aid to middle-income countries must be countered.

One rationale, seldom admitted by OECD governments, is that the emerging market economies are important markets for OECD products and so aid is useful in maintaining good relations with their governments. This is, of course, an abuse of aid. Were other, more legitimate sounding concerns of OECD governments properly addressed, this illegitimate rationale could be exposed and faced down. While recognising that it is a motive for aid, it is therefore important to attend to any rationales for providing aid to middle-income

There is a need both to sharpen the focus of ODA onto LDCs, and to look to alternatives.

... in an LDC poverty cannot be solved through redistribution: there is not enough national income to redistribute.

countries that appear superficially to be more legitimate. There are two such reasons why OECD donors do not allocate more of their aid to the LDCs.

One rationale for OECD aid to middle-income countries is that even middle-income countries have many poor people in them. This argument is spurious because a middle-income country is in a position to address such poverty from its own national income. If the government of a middle-income country chooses not to redistribute national income it should not expect other societies to address the poverty of its people with their own income. In contrast, in an LDC poverty cannot be solved through redistribution: there is not enough national income to redistribute.

The second, and more potent, rationale is that aid is better-used in middle-income countries because policies and institutions are better than in LDCs. The quality of policies and institutions is measured annually by the World Bank and published in its highly influential *Country Policy and Institutional Assessment* (CPIA). The CPIA formally determines the aid allocations of the World Bank and influences the allocations of many other donors. It is time that this approach to aid allocation was challenged. By linking the volume of aid to a country to its CPIA, LDCs almost inevitably end up with smaller aid allocations than middle-income countries. In particular, they get little of the fully discretionary funding that they need, such as is provided by budget support. In the donor perception there is a tension between the need for aid and the ability of governments to use it. This then faces donors with an impossible choice: provide aid to needy environments where it will be badly used, or provide it to environments where it will be better used but where it is not really needed.

The governments of LDCs need first to recognise that while donors feel that this is the choice with which they are faced, most major donors will tend to favour aid to middle-income countries. This is because their fiduciary responsibility to their own taxpayers leads them to be fearful of contexts in which aid can be shown to have been used badly. Looming fiscal pressures in OECD countries can only intensify such concerns and threaten to undermine provision of budget support. Having recognised the nature of the problem, governments of LDCs need then to do something about it. There are two approaches, potentially complementary.

One approach is to encourage independent assessment of the capacity of the government to spend aid honestly and effectively, such as is necessary for a donor to be confident that budget support will be properly used. The most appropriate agency would probably be the IMF, which already undertakes public financial management performance reports. However, currently these do not include an overall assessment as to whether a system is fit for budget support. *Were the IMF to certify systems as fit for budget support it would enormously strengthen the case for donors to provide it.* Indeed, it might even give the US Congress the evidence it claims is lacking to justify American provision of budget support. Evidently, not all LDCs are currently at a level of government capacity at which certification would be assured. Hence, it would be important to combine a certification process with transitional arrangements, including support for capacity building followed by re-assessment for those countries currently below the standard necessary for certification.

Another approach, which can potentially be complementary to certification, is for LDC governments to encourage routes by which aid can still be received by public agencies even if donors are unwilling to provide budget support directly into the budget. While from the perspective of government this may be inferior to budget support, it is evidently better than the government not receiving the aid at all.

> *zWere the IMF to certify systems as fit for budget support it would enormously strengthen the case for donors to provide it.*

At present, the main alternative modalities to budget support are project aid, the provision of aid directly to local governments (as with World Bank aid to Ethiopia) and completely bypassing government through direct donor funding of non-governmental organisations (NGOs). None of these are satisfactory. In particular, the NGO bypass undermines the capacity and authority of government.

Rather than merely oppose such approaches (which simply results in less aid), governments of LDCs can build new designs of public organisations which give donors sufficient confidence to provide finance, while retaining government control. One such approach is the public service agency (PSA) (Collier, 2009). A PSA is a government body which finances, but does not directly provide, public services such as health and education. It contracts with NGOs, local communities or local governments (according to what the government considers appropriate). As with an independent central bank, the government sets the rules and guidelines by which the PSA allocates the money received from donors. The PSA then finances the service providers (such as NGOs) on terms which it sets, and monitors their performance. Donors have representation in the management and oversight of the PSA (although the government retains overall control). However, since a core function of the PSA is to monitor the performance of the service providers, donors receive a continuous flow of information as to the cost-effectiveness of their aid. This gives them the confidence to provide enhanced funding.

PSAs need not be temporary arrangements. In many LDC contexts they may well turn out to be more cost-effective ways of providing public services than the conventional OECD model of direct government provision inherited by LDC governments at independence, which has often proved to be ill-suited to local conditions.

As with independent certification for budget support, the principle underlying public service agencies is for the governments of LDCs to recognise why for the past two decades they have been getting such a small share of global aid, and to address the problem by meeting the reasonable concerns of OECD governments.

Sharpening the focus of aid to LDCs on growth

The predominant original rationale for the millennium development goals (MDGs) was to strengthen the case for aid in OECD societies. In this they have been rather successful. However, their subsidiary rationale of shifting the priorities of LDC governments onto MDG-monitored outcomes, can potentially be counterproductive. In some LDC contexts the MDGs are manifestly not the most pressing priorities. For example, in post-conflict situations it is often important to generate jobs for young men as quickly as possible, yet employment is not an MDG.

More fundamentally, the MDGs are outcomes, rather than a strategy for achieving those outcomes. Inadvertently, the focus on the MDGs can create the impression than these desirable social outcomes, such as universal primary education, are simply purchased by aid. Yet the only sustainable way of achieving the MDGs and the myriad of other goals that a society aspires to, is through growth of the economy. Aid can potentially be helpful in financing the costs of growth, such as the necessary economic infrastructure. Yet the emphasis upon social goals risks diverting aid from such fundamental economic priorities to purposes which are more instantly appealing to voters in OECD countries. Over the past 15 years this has clearly occurred: funding for infrastructure has declined, while funding for social objectives has increased. As an example of uses of aid for enhanced growth, in Chapter 2 the case was made for aid to be used to finance

... the MDGs are outcomes, rather than a strategy for achieving those outcomes.

> ... it is timely for the governments of LDCs to insist on a refocusing of aid on a growth agenda.

prospecting for natural resources. An LDC where such a use of aid might be useful is Yemen, which is almost entirely dependent upon revenues from natural resources, but where proven reserves are near to exhaustion. There is a reasonable case for permitting the Government of Yemen to use some of its aid to finance exploration so that these revenues become more sustainable.

The international community is now starting to think beyond the time horizon of the MDGs. Hence, *it is timely for the governments of LDCs to insist on a refocusing of aid on a growth agenda.*

Rethinking debt sustainability

LDCs with IMF programmes were explicitly required not to borrow commercially. However, the IMF is now rethinking what determines debt sustainability and this is opening up the options for financing.

The model used by the IMF in its debt sustainability analysis implicitly assumed that public investment was completely unproductive. This followed from the lack of a link in the model from public investment to subsequent growth of the economy. Hence, by assumption, borrowing to finance extra public investment necessarily reduced the sustainability of debt: liabilities were incurred without any corresponding increase in productive assets.

These assumptions were clearly unreasonable. For example, the Growth Commission, led by Nobel Laureate Michael Spence, analysed all the countries that had transformed themselves from being low income and on the basis of its analysis urged LDCs to raise their rates of public investment. To its credit, the IMF is now revisiting its assumptions. In an important new working paper, 'Public Capital and Growth' by Arslanalp *et al.* (2010), the Fiscal Affairs Department of the IMF analyses the relationship between public investment and growth both in developing countries and in the OECD (where emerging debt crises raise the same issues that LDCs have grappled with for decades). The paper finds that public capital is productive but subject to diminishing returns. Beyond a certain level of the public capital stock further investment is unproductive and indeed can have net negative effects once the disincentive effects of the taxes needed to pay for it are taken into account.

Given the low level of public investment in LDCs in recent decades, many of them are likely to be within the range at which, on the IMF analysis, public investment is productive. As the paper notes, this has important implications for rethinking debt sustainability. Whereas in the old framework, borrowing for public investment necessarily worsened debt sustainability, once it is accepted that public investment can be productive, the effect of borrowing to finance it becomes contingent on what particular investments are being increased.

The critical issues become the rate of return on particular public investments, and whether sufficient of these returns can be captured through the tax system to enable the government to service the debt. While warranting some borrowing for public investment, the new perspective is not a licence to spend on whatever public capital is thought desirable. In particular, even though investments in social sectors, such as hospitals, may raise wellbeing, they may not sufficiently raise taxable income to be self-financing. Indeed, on the contrary, they may indirectly increase claims on public expenditure, most evidently through the recurrent costs necessary to operate the new capital. Borrowing for economic infrastructure is therefore the main candidate for expansion financed by borrowing.

What is needed to guard against debt becoming unsustainable is to base investment decisions on unbiased estimates of

Borrowing for economic infrastructure is therefore the main candidate for expansion financed by borrowing.

One approach might be for the World Bank to create an IBRD-like club of borrowers designed for LDCs.

the likely economic returns on marginal public investments. Both technically and politically this is difficult. Technically, the best that economics can offer is cost-benefit analysis, but this tends to be biased against large projects. Currently there are moves in some OECD countries towards setting up independent bureaux for budgetary assessment, and LDC governments may wish to build similar domestic institutions.

The new analysis is timely because the world is awash with liquidity. The rate of interest is at a historically low level, and the OECD countries are no longer seen automatically as safe havens. Further, as a result of the Jubilee campaign for debt forgiveness, most LDCs have very low levels of debt. Hence, there has seldom been a more propitious time for LDCs to increase the stock of public capital by borrowing commercially. Nevertheless, lending to LDCs is perceived as being high risk. It is therefore sensible to consider whether innovations in borrowing instruments can reduce the perceived risk of default.

Reducing the cost of commercial borrowing

One approach might be for the World Bank to *create an International Bank for Reconstruction and Development (IBRD)-like club of borrowers designed for LDCs*. When the IBRD was created, it was designed for countries that were not so different from LDCs today. Over the years, the IBRD club has, in effect, collectively moved up; in the process its members have become less risky and so are now able individually to borrow commercially. The IBRD club is not so necessary, other than at times of financial crisis. To contain risks, eligibility for membership of the IBRD-like club might be confined to those LDCs that were in conformity with an IMF programme or some such reassurance mechanism. The rationale for LDCs would be the same as that for the formation of the IBRD – by reducing perceived risk, it reduces the cost of borrowing. The IBRD carries a guarantee from OECD countries which has never been called. Unlike the International Development Association (IDA) it has therefore come at no fiscal cost. In the present environment of fiscal tightness in the OECD this is important. For example, it explains why at the March 2009 meeting of the G20, vast new resources were found for the IMF, while only negligible new money was found for the World Bank. Hence, a substantial expansion of financing for LDCs is more likely if it can use strategies which do not make explicit fiscal calls on the OECD.

A second approach, which might well be combined with the above, is for the rate of return on the bonds issued by LDCs to be linked to some aspect related to their ability to repay. That is, *it is better for objective risks to be shared explicitly rather than be left lurking as an offstage risk of default*. One performance measure is the rate of growth of GDP. This is a further advantage of a collective borrowing instrument such as an IBRD-like club, since the rate of interest on the bonds issued could be linked to the average growth rate of the LDC club. This would virtually eliminate the 'moral hazard' which would be associated with each individual government linking the rate of interest to the rate of growth of its own economy.

Another possible link is to the prices of commodity exports and imports. Potentially, the risks of commodity exporters can now be hedged. However, it would be unwise for LDC governments directly to engage in such transactions. Even the international investment banks have periodically proved incapable of adequately supervising their employees engaged in these transactions and have found themselves inadvertently exposed to massive losses. It is therefore preferable to have these risk transactions managed by a third party with expertise but no commercial interest, such as the World Bank. The Bank would undertake hedging operations on

> *A second approach ... is for the rate of return on the bonds issued by LDCs to be linked to some aspect related to their ability to repay. ... it is better for objective risks to be shared explicitly rather than be left lurking as an offstage risk of default.*

> *The legitimate rationales for public–private partnerships are either to finance new capital or to bring in superior management.*

behalf of LDC governments aimed at reducing the volatility of the revenues generated by rapid changes in the prices of commodity exports. While it is not realistic to aim at stabilising such revenues, it should be possible to slow the rates of change, softening periods of declining revenues by accepting a slower pace of price increase at times of rapid increases in world prices.

While hedging can be costly, the World Bank is in a position to do some of it purely through internal matched transactions which would effectively be cost free. For example, it could match portfolios of loans to oil exporters (whether or not these were LDCs) with loans to oil-importing LDCs. When oil prices were rising, debt service on the loans of oil-importers would be reduced and those of oil exporters correspondingly increased, and vice versa when oil prices fell.

A final link between returns and performance is to move the focus from the national level to the project level. Public–private partnerships provide security to investors by earmarking specified public assets collateral, while sharing the risk by linking debt service to certain verifiable aspects of the performance of the project. The recent Greek fiscal crisis has demonstrated how public–private partnerships can be abused. If the state merely shifts existing public assets into 'partnerships', it undermines the collateral for general public debt, increasing the risk of default. The legitimate rationales for public–private partnerships are either to finance new capital or to bring in superior management. In the former case, the new capital can indeed be used as collateral without undermining the collateral for existing debt. In the latter case, the right structure is either a management contract in which the private firm receives a specified return for improvements in performance while the state retains full ownership of the capital, or an outright sale of public assets (privatisation) rather than a partnership.

Increasing absorptive capacity for investment

While the IMF analysis on the returns on public capital is encouraging, it also finds that in developing countries public investment can become unproductive at surprisingly low levels of the public capital stock. This is support for the conventional IMF concern about constraints upon 'absorptive capacity'. If borrowing to finance public investment is to be viable on any scale, it is therefore essential to break this capacity constraint. Three approaches are complementary in raising the capacity to absorb public investment.

One approach is for government itself to improve its capacity to select and implement investments efficiently. As part of this it may be useful to establish an independent public institution for the scrutiny of proposed public investment projects. While cost-benefit analysis is technically the best way of selecting projects, it may require more capacity than many LDCs can reasonably muster, and it does not address issues of implementation. An alternative or supplement to cost-benefit analysis is to learn from the success of countries that two decades ago were themselves LDCs but which, through rapid growth, have transformed themselves. The government of an LDC could decide to follow the scale and sequence of public investment projects that had been carried out by a country that two decades ago was similar, but which has grown rapidly. For example, such a peer-matching exercise may reveal that heavy investment in rural areas is less important than investment in urban infrastructure: after two decades of rapid growth, cities are where the population and the economy are predominantly located. *Formalising opportunities for such learning from former peer countries would be helpful to the governments of LDCs.*

The second approach is to adopt policies that are conducive to private investment. Public and private investments are complementary, implying that the return on public

An alternative ... is to learn from the success of countries that two decades ago were themselves LDCs but which, through rapid growth, have transformed themselves.

Public and private investments are seldom substitutes: usually they are complementary

investment depends in part upon the level of private investment. There are already various international ratings of investment policies which can be helpful to the governments of LDCs in guiding policy reform. For example, Rwanda has recently risen dramatically in these ratings.

The third approach is to focus on policies which reduce the cost of capital goods, both structures and equipment. Both types of capital good tend to be more expensive in LDCs than in other countries, so that an expenditure on investment buys less capital. Bringing down the cost of structures is a matter of targeting construction costs. These can be excessive for many different reasons: legal impediments on the acquisition of urban land, bottlenecks in the supply of cement or shortages of skilled labour. Each of these problems can be addressed by appropriate policies. Bringing down the cost of equipment depends upon trade policy, because in LDCs equipment is imported. If the market in imported equipment is merely national, in an LDC it will inevitably be small. Small markets are unlikely to support enough importers to be competitive. Instead, they will be characterised by cartels and prices set above world levels (Collier and Venables, 2010b). A good way around this problem is to encourage markets in equipment to be organised regionally rather than nationally; this in turn depends upon the removal of trade barriers within the region. Collectively, these three approaches to increasing absorptive capacity are an agenda for 'investing-in-investing'.

Innovations in financing private investment

In many LDCs the ratio of private capital to public capital is lower than in more developed economies. Public and private investments are seldom substitutes: usually they are complementary. Private investment finances activities that are not well suited to be managed by government. Hence, many

LDCs are even more lacking in private investment than they are in public investment. Much of the finance for private investment in LDCs will need to be foreign, and so the challenge is to attract it in various forms. Some forms are better than others. Short-term foreign private lending to commercial banks has proved to be fickle and therefore dangerous. At the other end of the spectrum of private financing, foreign direct investment is not readily reversible and also brings skills and networks. The third main form of private finance is the purchase of equity in domestic firms. This is attractive because it is risk bearing, so that LDCs can share some of the risks they face.

Foreign investment in the private sector in LDCs is perceived as risky and this is an important deterrent. There are various ways in which these perceived risks can be reduced.

Foreign investment in the private sector in LDCs is perceived as risky and this is an important deterrent.

Investment standards

For FDI one approach is for governments of LDCs to commit to certain standards of conduct which protect the investor against uncompensated confiscation. Most governments now have investment codes. However, these provide only limited reassurance because as purely national standards they can readily be changed unilaterally by governments. This is an example of a problem which has become standard in economics, known as 'time-inconsistency'. Governments (or indeed firms) which lack the ability to make commitments which are fully credible to other parties find that they are unable to make some deals which would be mutually attractive and so lose out. The key insight of the 'time-consistency' analysis is that faced with such situations governments themselves gain from placing credible restraints on their own power. LDC governments face precisely this problem vis-à-vis FDI and so would gain from appropriate ways of placing restraints on their individual power to confiscate private

> [LDCs] should collectively propose a common standard for foreign investment to which they are willing to adhere.

investment. Agreed international standards of conduct can be useful for the governments of LDCs in providing such restraints, although they must be standards set and agreed by LDC governments themselves, rather than imposed on them externally. In the 1990s the OECD attempted to create an international investment code to which LDCs were supposed to subscribe. This was precisely the wrong way to address the problem. Inadvertently, it created the impression that the OECD was attempting to force LDCs to accept standards that they were unwilling to adopt themselves. The collapse of this initiative left LDCs in a worse position than they had been before: by opposing the OECD proposal they were made to appear as wanting to confiscate foreign investment. Since then there has been no new initiative. Sufficient time has passed since that mistaken attempt for a new approach to be worthwhile. *This time the initiative should come from LDC governments themselves. They should collectively propose a common standard for foreign investment to which they are willing to adhere.* The proposal should include arrangements for independent adjudication to settle disputes and enforcement procedures for decisions. A common, enforced standard has two advantages. One, as discussed above, is the greater credibility of an international standard than of purely national codes. The other is that a common standard guards against a race-to-the-bottom in which international firms attempt to play off competing LDC governments.

Attracting foreign equity

LDCs are high-risk environments and the main financial instrument for financing in the context of high risks is equity. Yet to date LDCs have attracted very little foreign equity into their firms. Various public vehicles for purchasing the equity of firms in developing countries exist, such as the CDC and the International Finance Corporation (IFC).

However, to date, they have shied away from investment in LDCs. The governments of LDCs could usefully lobby for an increased share of these portfolios. This would be timely, since World Bank President Robert Zoellick has proposed that sovereign wealth funds should set a target of investing 1 per cent of their portfolios in low-income Africa. An evident generalisation of this proposal would be for the target group to be defined as LDCs. Since SWFs are becoming major vehicles for saving by EMEs, it is important to establish some link between them and the finance of investment in the poorest countries. It would be politically advantageous to link these two desired portfolio shifts. The one, through instruments such as the IFC and CDC, is through entities which are predominantly OECD financed. The other, through SWFs, is predominantly EME financed. Linking them would gear up the benefits to each decision and so increase the chances of each being adopted.

Remittances are now a major source of finance for LDCs. However, they are almost entirely a flow of money to households to enable increases in the consumption of imports.

Innovations in remittances

Remittances are now a major source of finance for LDCs. However, they are almost entirely a flow of money to households to enable increases in the consumption of imports. To the extent that remittances come from long-term migrants they are unsustainable, liable to dwindle as links with the country of origin fade across generations and as immigration restrictions in OECD countries are tightened. They therefore carry the classic Dutch disease risk of temporarily appreciating the real exchange rate and thereby undermining the process of industrialisation.

To counter this adverse effect of remittances, one approach is for the government to capture some of them so that some of the flow can finance public investment instead of only private consumption. Some governments, such as Egypt and Pakistan, have adapted domestic financial institutions so as to encourage migrants to hold large balances domestically. The banks can then hold some of these in the form of government bonds. Potentially, governments could also attempt to tax remittances: technically this is becoming easier as remitters rely more and more upon electronic transfers.

Complementary to governments capturing some of the flow, would be a switch in the composition of migration from permanent to temporary (Mode 4). Temporary migration addresses the risk that remittances will dwindle as the ties with emigrants weaken and may also be politically acceptable to OECD societies. A potential deal with OECD governments is that LDC governments agree to accept back some of the stock of illegal migrants in return for a generous but controlled flow of legal temporary migration.

The really big potential gain would be to link the switch to temporary migration to the need for the government to capture revenue from migrants. Thus, if migration was both temporary and legally controlled, it would be administratively feasible to require migrants to make minimum tax payments to their own governments as a condition for continued rights of residence in host countries. An analogy is the tax that the Government of Eritrea successfully levied on emigrants living in OECD countries as a condition for passport renewal.

6 Climate Change, Asian Growth and Food Security in LDCs

In low-income countries, food is half of the expenditure of ordinary people. Food security is therefore fundamental to their wellbeing. To date, the main source of food insecurity in LDCs has come from variations in domestic production consequent upon climatic shocks. However, many LDCs are already net importers of food and as their populations urbanise in coastal cities, a growing proportion of their populations will become dependent upon imported food rather than domestic production. This exposes LDCs to a further source of food insecurity, namely shocks to world supply resulting in periods of very high prices.

With the rapid growth of food consumption in the emerging market economies, world food markets are continuously being stretched to meet rising demand. Accentuating this long-term trend towards tighter market conditions, increased climatic volatility is periodically exposing one or other of the major grain-producing regions to shocks that hit output.

In response to such shocks, food prices rise to squeeze down consumption to meet reduced world supply. Food-exporting countries protect themselves from this effect by banning grain exports, as is currently the case in Ukraine. This compounds the problem for food importers. Inevitably, the poorest consumers are the ones who are priced out, and so a world food crisis affects LDCs much more severely than most other countries. The food crisis of 2008 was an instance of such a shock. The emerging global food crisis of 2010 brings together climatic shocks and global sourcing of food. The climatic shock has been a severe drought in Russia. But because Russia is a major global producer, the consequences of the shock are being felt in the coastal cities of LDCs.

... as their [LDCs'] populations urbanise in coastal cities, a growing proportion of their populations will become dependent upon imported food rather than domestic production.

CATCHING UP: WHAT LDCS CAN DO, AND HOW OTHERS CAN HELP

[LDCs'] agenda on climate change should predominantly be about adaptation rather than mitigation.

Exposure through climate change

LDCs are thus doubly exposed to global warming: through deterioration in their own climates and through shocks in major food producers. Yet, for the next half century the climate is set to deteriorate both globally and especially in LDCs. This is going to happen regardless of whether further carbon emissions are satisfactorily curtailed, since the lags between the flow of new emissions and the stock of carbon dioxide in the atmosphere are very long. The climate is set to deteriorate because emissions during the period 1960–2010 were much higher than those during 1910–1960. Beyond 2060 the climate facing LDCs is likely to deteriorate further because of delays in curtailing the future emissions of the industrialised and industrialising parts of the world.

The above facts have an obvious but neglected implication for LDCs: their own agenda on climate change should predominantly be about adaptation rather than mitigation. The rest of the world should have the opposite priority. In the OECD and the EMEs the climate is generally not as hot as in LDCs and so it is not set to deteriorate as much. Further, their economies are not as exposed to changes in climate because they are less dependent upon rain-fed agriculture. While they therefore have less need for adaptation, both the OECD and the EMEs urgently need to curb their emissions. Hence for them mitigation, rather than adaptation, should be the priority.

This fundamental difference in priorities is in danger of being missed because so much of the global discourse on climate change is, in effect, a dispute between the OECD countries and the EMEs as to who should do what on mitigation. EMEs want the OECD to pay for the mitigation they undertake, while OECD countries wish to minimise their own costs. It has been tempting for LDCs to insert themselves as a third party to this dispute, seeking compensation from the OECD for their own costs of adaptation and mitigation. However, within the terms of this dispute the overwhelming interest of LDCs is in getting both the OECD and the EMEs to do as much mitigation as possible, rather than to extract as much money as possible. Given the financial constraints on OECD budgets, the bulk of the 'compensation' that LDCs receive for the costs of adaptation is likely, indirectly, to come from OECD aid budgets. LDCs have no effective way of preventing the switch from aid to compensation because OECD countries will not make it explicit: indeed, faced with the charge, they will explicitly deny any link, yet aid budgets will wither as compensation payments rise. LDCs will thus be compensating themselves, while in the process becoming subjected to a new wave of conditionality, this time environmental. Such environmental conditionality brings dangers: it could potentially force LDCs to meet higher standards than the OECD and EMEs are willing to impose on themselves. For example, there are already indications that aid may be withheld from opening coal deposits in LDCs, whereas coalmining is still being expanded in both OECD countries and EMEs. As the main sufferers from continued climatic deterioration, LDCs have a natural authority in trying to broker an agreement between the main remitters. It may not be worth jeopardising this role by insisting on a compensation agenda which is unlikely to be realised.

Potentially, LDCs may be able to make some money from selling mitigation. However, even here there are severe limits. To date, the Clean Development Mechanism has overwhelmingly benefited the EMEs, and particularly China, rather than LDCs. This is partly because, given their rapid industrialisation, the EMEs have many more opportunities for mitigation, and partly because they are better placed to meet the governance standards for mitigation to be verified and certified.

... the overwhelming interest of LDCs is in getting both the OECD and the EMEs to do as much mitigation as possible, rather than to extract as much money as possible.

The key innovation in the science of improving crop varieties has been genetic modification (GM).

Turning to the adaptation agenda, which should be the priority of LDCs, this has two components. The sector most adversely affected by climate change is agriculture. Hence, one aspect of adaptation is to reduce the exposure of agriculture to climate change: the other is to reduce the exposure of LDC economies to agriculture.

Adaptation within agriculture

Agriculture is exposed to climate change because the plants that are grown in each LDC are, by a long process of selection, adapted to grow best in the climatic conditions that are currently prevailing. Hence, for most countries *any* change in climate is likely to worsen growing conditions until plants adapt. Further, climate change seems likely to increase climatic volatility, with more extreme temperatures, floods and droughts. Plants will therefore be stressed beyond the range of climate in which they can readily survive. Over time plants adapt: the varieties grown in LDCs have changed considerably over the centuries. However, if climate change is rapid, there is a danger that the pace of adaptation achieved by past methods will not be able to keep abreast of it. Hence, there is a need to speed up crop adaptation. The pace of crop adaptation depends on the speed of innovation in crop varieties and how rapidly these new varieties spread among farmers: that is, on research and extension.

The key innovation in the science of improving crop varieties has been genetic modification (GM). There is a strong case for supporting research on GM with public money. Instead, paradoxically, many LDCs, notably in Africa, have banned the adoption of GM. The impetus for this ban was the ban imposed by Europe in 1996. In political terms the European ban is most reasonably interpreted as a standard piece of agricultural protectionism, although as is usual with such protectionism a smokescreen was used, in this case a health scare. Europe's own scientific authorities have, however, found no health basis for the ban. As European grain productivity falls progressively further behind that of North America, it seems increasingly likely that the ban will be relaxed, probably country by country. Meanwhile there is a strong case for LDC governments to lift their own bans. Until this is done, GM research on the crops best suited for LDC conditions will not even get started.

Agricultural extension services are organisationally difficult, in part because the performance of staff is hard to monitor. In many LDCs extension services have deteriorated, partly due to chronic underfunding. However, it is not clear that low agricultural productivity is primarily due to farmer ignorance, nor that extension is an effective way of spreading knowledge. It may be more cost effective to use limited public funds to accelerate crop research than to try to rebuild extension services which have proved to be so problematic. However, agriculture is highly location specific and so this choice does not lend itself to generalisation.

If food cannot reliably be produced domestically due to climatic shocks, then the economy needs to develop export activities that are not climate sensitive and which can therefore pay for imported food.

Adaptation between sectors

If LDC agriculture is set to become more subject to climatic shocks, it is sensible also to try to reduce the exposure of LDC economies to domestic agriculture. If food cannot reliably be produced domestically due to climatic shocks, then the economy needs to develop export activities that are not climate sensitive and which can therefore pay for imported food. The larger and more diversified a country's exports, the less vulnerable it is to shocks in domestic food production and the better it can cope with price shocks in global food markets. For most LDCs the options for the expansion of exports are natural resources (as discussed in Chapter 2) and light manufactures (as discussed in Chapter 3). There is also sometimes potential for the export of e-services. Here the key inputs are typically good international telecoms and a good post-primary education system, neither of which are currently adequate in most LDCs. It is important that LDCs do not get stuck with new environmental conditionality that makes it more difficult for them to diversify their economies out of agriculture.

Reducing the risks from global food shocks

There is little that LDCs can do to reduce the risk of global food shocks, but since LDCs bear the brunt of the consequences, it is worth lobbying for policy improvements in other countries. There are three key actions by other countries that would reduce risks. First, the USA has reduced global food supply through its subsidies for grain used as biofuel. The subsidies inadvertently worsen food insecurity in LDCs. Second, in 1996 the EU banned genetically modified organisms (GMOs). This has reduced productivity growth in European grain production and so again reduced global food supply. It has also impeded Africa from adopting GMOs because of fears of restrictions on African exports. Third, several food-exporting EMEs have imposed export bans at times of high world prices in order to protect their domestic consumers. This is a damaging beggar-thy-neighbour policy. In the short term it pushes prices up further, and in the longer term it reduces agricultural investment in these EMEs and so reduces world supply. Concern over export bans has prompted Ngozi Okonjo-Iweala, Managing Director of the World Bank, to speak out against the current grain export ban by Ukraine. Collectively, LDC governments have the authority to condemn the above polices. The major players in the international community should not get away with paying lip-service to concerns about food insecurity while adopting policies that deepen the problem.

Complementary to advocating policies that raise global

The major players in the international community should not get away with paying lip-service to concerns about food insecurity while adopting policies that deepen the problem.

food production are policies that raise food productivity in LDCs themselves. One such policy, the adoption of GMOs, has been noted above. However, other new policies could also be adopted. For decades LDC governments have attempted to raise the productivity of peasant agriculture. One lesson from these past efforts is that this approach is difficult. In contrast, some EMEs, such as Brazil, have successfully raised agricultural production through the expansion of commercial agriculture. The process of growing crops in the ground is not itself subject to scale economies. However, as agricultural productivity becomes more dependent upon technology, purchased inputs and logistics, commercial organisation starts to have advantages over small-scale farming. There is now strong evidence that small farms are less productive than larger farms. Some LDCs have underutilised land which could be opened to commercial farming on a competitive basis. However, such commercial operations are quite distinct from the geopolitical mega-deals that some governments have attempted to negotiate with LDCs. Such deals are aimed to pre-empt food supplies from the global market so as to achieve food security in the countries that acquire these large tracts of land. They are disadvantageous to LDCs: being non-commercial operations there is no reason to expect that the farming practices they adopt will be efficient. Further, since their rationale is to pre-empt LDC food production at times of global shortage, they worsen LDC food insecurity.

7 Conclusion

The post-boom global economy looks to have some important differences with the half-century since LDC independence. As other developing countries rapidly converge on a crisis-ridden OECD, LDCs are becoming increasingly distinctive. The OECD economies are in crisis and so aid is set to decline relative to the GDP of LDCs: new types of international finance for LDCs will need to be developed. Because other developing countries are growing rapidly, commodity prices are likely to remain high, making the management of natural resources critical, and LDCs will have a chance of being competitive in labour-intensive manufacturing, making pump-priming industrial policies valuable.

Supportive international policies need to be sharply differentiated so that LDCs can begin to converge on the rest of mankind. Yet no international agency has either a remit focused on the poorest countries or a mandate that spans all the different types of policy. Nor are LDCs adequately represented in the G8/G20 process, to which the EMEs have now gained entry. This makes it imperative that the governments of LDCs collectively take leadership of the pertinent agenda. It may be helpful to summarise the international agenda suggested in this paper.

Supportive international policies need to be sharply differentiated so that LDCs can begin to converge on the rest of mankind.

The International Agenda: a Summary

Harnessing natural resources for development:

1. In view of the overarching importance of resource extraction for most LDCs in the coming decade, it would be helpful for LDC governments collectively to endorse common guidelines for their management, such as the guidelines set out in the independent Natural Resource Charter.

2. Aid to finance public geological information. This would enable LDC governments both to attract companies and to reduce the information gap between governments and companies. The US Government recently provided this to the Government of Afghanistan.

3. A new voluntary international standard for encouraging and policing competition in awarding contracts for resource extraction through auctions, in order to gain maximum benefit to governments.

4. The WTO to provide commitment mechanisms for LDC governments wishing to reduce the perceived risk of resource extraction contracts.

5. The international financial institutions (IFIs) substantially to scale up their provision of advice on resource taxation to governments of LDCs. The pay-off for good professional advice is very high because resource extraction companies are expert at minimising tax bills. But the cost of such advice on the open market is beyond the means of LDCs.

6. Where an LDC government prefers to sell resource extraction rights directly in exchange for a package of infrastructure and aid (as in Chinese deals), other donor governments should comply with this preference by putting together equivalent consortia which could compete.

7. Within the WTO, defend the right to impose local content rules for purposes of promoting diversification.

8. Ask the WTO to impose on all its member countries the requirement recently imposed by the Lugar-Cardin Amendment on those companies listed on the New York Stock Exchange.

9. Develop an international capability for dispute resolution in cases of environmental damage caused by resource extraction, through which adversely affected local communities can appeal for fair and enforced compensation.

Breaking in to manufacturing

10. Establish a common preference scheme for those LDCs that have yet to break into manufactures, with generous ROO (analogous to the AGOA garment rules). At a minimum the OECD countries should provide a common scheme for privileged market access, but much better would be for a common global scheme brokered by the G20, under which the emerging market economies also provided privileged market access for LDC products.

Promoting urbanisation

11. Donors need to shift their priorities from a somewhat romantic rural-social agenda which has dominated the past decade, to a more practical urban-economic agenda which is where future development will take place. It will be much easier for donors to make this change if it is a collective demand of LDC governments rather than case-by-case appeals.

Rebuilding foreign financing

12. Donors should change their basis for aid allocation so that proportionately more aid goes to LDCs.

13. The international agencies, and particularly the IMF, should extend their public expenditure and financial accountability (PEFA) assessments so as to be able formally to certify budget systems as fit for aid in the form of budget support, so that aid can be reallocated from projects and special purpose funds.

14. In those environments in which NGOs play a significant role in the delivery of basic services, the World Bank should be encouraged to develop new administrative arrangements for aid delivery, along the lines of public service agencies, which enable governments to control and co-ordinate NGO activities.

15. The World Bank should be asked to develop an IBRD-2 scheme for pre-emerging market economies, whereby over and above the IDA, governments could borrow at close to the risk-free world commercial interest rate.

16. LDC governments should initiate a global investment guarantee scheme, designed on their terms, so as to reduce the high risk-premium which they currently pay for foreign investment.

17. LDC governments should support and invigorate the Zoellick initiative on target shares of sovereign wealth funds being invested in LDCs.

18. Lobby for a switch from permanent and uncontrolled migration to temporary and controlled migration to OECD countries. Ideally this would be linked to a mechanism for generating revenue for government.

Promoting food security in the face of climate change

19. In LDCs the key climate change issue is adaptation, whereas in developed and emerging market economies it is mitigation. Hence, assistance to LDCs should be for adaptation rather than mitigation.

20. Adaptation within agriculture needs rapid innovation in crop varieties and GMOs are a useful mechanism for such innovation. LDC governments should encourage public research on GMOs in developed countries. As part of this governments should lift bans on GMOs.

21. LDC governments should support the concern of Ngozi Okonjo-Iweala that food-exporting countries should refrain from banning exports.

While the international agenda has been the core focus of this paper, supportive domestic policies in LDCs may also need to be reprioritised. During the past decade they have been social and rural, often heavily influenced by donor preferences. Yet future economic opportunities will be predominantly urban and will require supporting infrastructure and market integration. Market integration will require a far more effective approach to regional integration than LDC governments have had to date. It is most likely to come not from the pan-regional approach (because too many governments are involved), but from small groups of neighbouring countries (such as the East African Community) with strong common interests. Many LDCs are landlocked. Landlocked countries have a vital interest in cost-effective transport corridors. These require both hard and soft infrastructure. The hard infrastructure involves large fixed investments across borders; attracting such investment therefore depends upon effectively eliminating the multiple opportunities for hold-up inherent in unlimited sovereign rights. The soft infrastructure involves curtailing the corruption which is parasitic on the flow of commerce.

Notes

1. Both the EU and USA also have regional integration agreements extending preferences on a reciprocal basis, and the EU is moving towards replacing its Cotonou agreements with such Economic Partnership Agreements. Our focus is on unilateral rather than reciprocal preferences, although some of our policy messages will apply to both.
2. Hoekman *et al.* (2006), drawing on Low *et al.* (2005). See also Olarreaga and Özden (2005) for an application to preferences in the apparel sector.
3. Computable general equilibrium studies of trade preferences include both rent and supply effects, but typically ignore the potential of scale thresholds. See Bchir *et al.* (2007) for a recent example.
4. See Duranton and Puga (2005) for a survey of the micro-economic mechanisms underlying clustering.
5. For further development of these ideas see Burgess and Venables (2004) and Puga and Venables (1996).
6. See Rodrik (2004) for discussion of these issues.
7. For details of eligibility see http://www.agoa.gov/eligibility/country_eligibility.html.

References

Arslanalp, S, Bornhorst, F, Gupta, S and Sze, E (2010). 'Public Capital and Growth', IMF Working Paper 10/175.

Bchir, M, Karingi, SN, Mold, A, Osakwe, PN and Jallab, MS (2007). 'The Doha Development Round and Africa: Partial and General Equilibrium Analyses of Tariff Preference Erosion', *Agricultural Economics*, 37(s1), December: 287–295.

Bevan, DL, Collier, P and Gunning, JW (1999). *Poverty, Equity and Growth in Nigeria and Indonesia*, Oxford University Press, New York.

Burgess, R and Venables, AJ (2004). 'Toward a Microeconomics of Growth', Policy Research Working Paper Series 3257, World Bank, Washington, DC.

Collier, P (2009). 'Rethinking the Provision of Public Services in Post-Conflict States' in *Partnership for Democratic Governance Contracting Out Government Functions and Services: Emerging Lessons from Post-Conflict and Fragile Situations*, OECD Development, vol. 21, no. 21: 115–122.

Collier, P (2010). *The Plundered Planet: How to Reconcile Prosperity with Nature*, Penguin, London.

Collier, P and Venables, AJ (2007). 'Rethinking Trade Preferences: How Africa Can Diversify its Exports', *The World Economy*, 30: 1326–1345.

Collier, P and Venables, AJ (2010a). 'International Rules for Trade in Natural Resources', *Journal of Globalization and Development*, 1(1).

Collier, P and Venables, AJ (2010b). 'Trade and Economic Performance: Does Africa's Fragmentation Matter?' in Lin and Pleskovic (eds), *Annual World Bank Conference on Development Economics (Global)*, World Bank, Washington, DC.

Collier, P, van der Ploeg, R, Spence, M and Venables, AJ (2010). 'Managing Resource Revenues in Developing Economies', IMF Staff Papers, *Palgrave Macmillan Journals*, 57(1): 84–118.

Duranton, G and Diego, P (2005). 'From Sectoral to Functional Urban Specialisation', *Journal of Urban Economics*, Elsevier, 57(2): 343–370.

Hausmann, R, Pritchett, L and Rodrik, D (2005). 'Growth Accelerations', *Journal of Economic Growth*, 10(4): 303–329.

Hausmann, R and Rodrik, D (2003). 'Economic Development as Self-discovery', *Journal of Development Economics*, 72(2): 603–633.

Hoekman, BM, Martin, WJ and Braga, P (2006). 'Preference Erosion: The Terms of the Debate' in Newfarmer, R (ed.), *Trade, Doha, and Development*, World Bank, Washington, DC.

Jones, B and Olken, B (2006). 'The Anatomy of Start-Stop Growth', NBER Working Paper No. 11528, National Bureau of Economic Research, Cambridge, Mass., USA.

Low, P, Piermartini, R and Richtering, J (2005). *Multilateral Solutions to the Erosion of Non-reciprocal Preferences in NAMA*, WTO, Geneva.

Olarreaga, M and Özden, Ç (2005). 'AGOA and Apparel: Who Captures the Tariff Rent in the Presence of Preferential Market Access?', *The World Economy*, 28(1): 63–77.

Pattillo, C, Gupta, S and Carey, K (2005). 'Sustaining Growth Accelerations and Pro-poor Growth in Africa', IMF Working Paper 05/195.

Puga, D and Venables, AJ (1996). 'The Spread of Industry: Spatial Agglomeration in Economic Development', *Journal of the Japanese and International Economies*, 10(4): 440–464.

Rodrik, D (2004). 'Industrial Policy for the Twenty-First Century', Working Paper Series rwp04-047, Harvard University, John F Kennedy School of Government, Cambridge, Mass., USA.

Subramanian, A and Roy, D (2003). 'Who Can Explain the Mauritian Miracle', in Rodrik, D (ed.), *In Search of Prosperity*, Princeton University Press, Princeton, NJ, USA.

Teravaninthorn, S and Raballand, G. (2008), *Transport Prices and Cost in Africa: A Review of the Main International Corridors*, World Bank, Washington, DC.

UNIDO (2009). *Industrial Development Report, Breaking In and Moving Up: New Industrial Challenges for the Bottom Billion and the Middle-Income Countries*, United Nations Industrial Development Organization, Vienna, Austria.

Index

absolute income differentials 1
absorptive capacity, investment 53–4
adaptation 60–4
　within agriculture 62–3
　between sectors 63–4
Africa
　manufacturing 19, 26, 28–32
　sovereign wealth funds 57
　transport sector 39
African Growth and Opportunities Act (AGOA) 19, 29–32
'agency' problem 12
AGOA see African Growth and Opportunities Act
agriculture
　climate change 62–5
　diminishing returns 20
　extension services 63
　hold-up problem 40–1
protectionism 62–3
aid
　allocation of 43–7
　vs compensation 61
　for economic growth 47–8
　multilateral 6–7
　social outcomes 47
Andean Trade Promotion Act 19
anti-bribery legislation 12, 13
apparel industry 30–1
Asian growth 4, 21, 59–65
asset choices 14–16
asymmetric information 6
auctions, natural resources 7–8, 10

Bangladesh 24
banking sector 39
　see also World Bank
barriers to trade 25, 35–6
best practice models 14–15
bidding at auctions 7, 10
Birdsall, Nancy 33
bonds 51
borrowing 48–52
Bourguignon, François 33
BP oil spill 11
bribery 12, 13
budget support 45–7

capacity assessment
　aid allocation 45
　investment funds 53–4
capital goods 39–40, 54
Caribbean Basin Initiative (CBI) 19
catalytic trade policies 21, 25–6
CBI (Caribbean Basin Initiative) 19
CDC (Commonwealth Development Corporation) 56–7
centralisation of revenues 11–12
certification process, aid 45
Chad–Cameroon pipeline project 14–15
China 9, 10, 36–7
city size
　productivity and 23–4, 36–8
　scale economies 35
Clean Development Mechanism 61
climate change 4, 59–65, 70–1
clustering 23–4, 30–2
commercial borrowing 50–2
commitment credibility 8–9, 55–6
commodity prices 5, 51–2
Commonwealth Development Corporation (CDC) 56–7
companies
　competition between 7
　environmental damage 11
　see also firm-level effects
comparative advantage 22, 24
compensation, climate change 60–1
competition
　between companies 7
　regional integration 38–41
complementary inputs 21–3
congestion costs 37
consumption standards 15
co-ordination failure 25, 41
corporate corruption 12–14
corruption 12–14
cost-benefit analysis 53
cost reductions
　capital goods 54
　commercial borrowing 50–2
　manufacturing 25–6
Cotonou agreement 19, 29
Country Policy and Institutional Assessment (CPIA) 44
credibility of commitments 8–9, 55–6
crop adaptation 62–3
crude oil 13

debt sustainability 48–52
developed countries 2
　see also individual countries
developing countries
　economic growth 1–3
　industrialisation 4
　see also individual countries
development finance 4, 43–58
diamond trade 13
diminishing returns to scale 20
Dispute Settlement Boards Mechanism 9
diversification 10
domestic policies 30, 71
donor confidence, aid allocation 44–6
'Dutch disease' 15–16, 57

EBA see Everything but Arms scheme
Economic Community of West African States (ECOWAS) 26
economic growth
　2000–2008 1–3
　aid for 47–8
　interest rate link 51
　manufacturing role 21, 24
economic partnership agreements (EPAs) 32–3
ECOWAS (Economic Community of West African States) 26
EITI see Extractive Industries Transparency Initiative
emerging market economies (EMEs)
　aid allocation 43
　climate change 60–1, 64–5
　G8/G20 process 67
　manufacturing markets 35
　market access 33
employment creation 20
environmental damage 11–12
　see also climate change
EPAs (economic partnership agreements) 32–3
EPZs (export processing zones) 31
Equatorial Guinea 2
equipment costs 54
equity risk 56–7
Eritrea 58
European Union (EU)
　agricultural protectionism 62–3
　trade preference schemes 19, 29–30, 32–3, 72
Everything but Arms (EBA) scheme 19, 29–30, 32
exchange rate spikes 16

export processing zones (EPZs) 31
exports
　adaptation 63–4
　commercial borrowing 51
　'Dutch disease' 15–16
　manufacturing 28, 31
　natural resources 5
　supply response 20–1
exposure to climate change 60–4
extension services, agriculture 63
Extractive Industries Transparency Initiative (EITI) 12, 17

farm size productivity 65
FDI (foreign direct investment) 55–6
finance
　for development 4, 43–58
　foreign finance 16, 55–7, 69–70
　see also aid; investment
firm-level effects 28, 38–41
　see also companies
food security 4, 59–65, 70–1
foreign direct investment (FDI) 55–6
foreign finance
　attracting 55–7
　'Dutch disease' avoidance 16
　rebuilding 69–70
fragmentation of production 22–5, 28

G8/G20 process 67
Generalised System of Preferences (GSP) 19
genetic modification (GM) 62–3, 64–5
geological information 6–7
global warming see climate change
global scale
　food shocks 64–5
　manufacturing system 19–33
GM see genetic modification
governance measures 1
governments of LDCs 67
　capacity assessment 45, 53
　company competition 7
　corporate corruption measures 14
　credible commitments 8–9, 55–6
　local content procurement rules 10
　manufacturing schemes 24–33
　Natural Resource Charter 17
　prospecting rights 6
　PSA approach 46–7
　remittance innovations 57–8

strategic policies 3–4
transparency mechanisms 12
growth
  economic 1–3, 21, 24, 47–8, 51
  population 37–8
Growth Commission 48
GSP (Generalised System of Preferences) 19
Guinea 2, 8

hard infrastructure 71
hedging operations 51–2
hold-up problem 23, 40–1

IBRD (International Bank for Reconstruction and Development) 50–1
ICRG (International Country Risk Guide) 1
IDA (International Development Association) 51
IFC (International Finance Corporation) 56–7
IMF see International Monetary Fund
imports, commercial borrowing 51
income consumption 15
income differentials 1–2, 39
increasing returns to scale 23–4
Indonesia 16
industrialisation 4, 25, 27, 35–6
infant mortality 1
infrastructure 10, 24–5, 47, 71
innovations in finance 43–58
integration schemes 4, 35–42, 71–2
interest groups, natural resources 16–17
interest rates, bonds 51
International Agenda summary 67–71
International Bank for Reconstruction and Development (IBRD) 50–1
international co-operation, corporate corruption 12–14
International Country Risk Guide (ICRG) 1
International Development Association (IDA) 51
International Finance Corporation (IFC) 56–7
International Monetary Fund (IMF)
  aid allocation 45
  debt sustainability 48–9
  IBRD approach 50–1
international standards, natural resources 17
investment
  absorptive capacity 53–4
  debt sustainability 48–50, 52
  innovations 54–7

natural resources 14–15
risks 9, 23, 40–1, 55
standards 55–6

Jubilee campaign 50
judicial systems 11

Kimberley Process 12–13
Kuwait 14–15

labour costs 26
landlocked countries 71
least developed countries (LDCs), membership categories 2
legislation
  money laundering 12
  pan-OECD anti-bribery legislation 12, 13
local content procurement rules 10, 68
local violence 11–12
Lugar-Cardin Amendment 13, 68

manufacturing
  breaking into 69
  hold-up problem 41
  modern sector production 22–4, 28
  policy implementation 21, 25–6, 30
  regional integration 35–6
  trade preference schemes 19–33
  see also production fragmentation; productivity levels
market access 19–20, 31–3
market integration 35, 71
market size 35–6, 37–41
Mauritius 28–9
MDGs (millennium development goals) 47–8
MFA see multi-fibre agreement
middle-income countries, aid 43–5
migration 58
millennium development goals (MDGs) 47–8
mitigation for climate change 60–1
modern sector production 22–4, 28
money laundering legislation 12
monopoly power 38–41
multi-fibre agreement (MFA) 29, 30
multilateral aid 6–7

Natural Resource Charter 17, 67
natural resource extraction 4, 5–17, 48, 67–9
NGOs see non-governmental organisations
Nigeria 13, 16

non-governmental organisations (NGOs) 46, 70
Norway 14–15

ODA (official development assistance) 43–7
OECD *see* Organisation for Economic
  Co-operation and Development
official development assistance (ODA) 43–7
oil
  BP spill 11
  hedging operations 52
  Lugar-Cardin Amendment 13
opportunities 4, 5–6
Organisation for Economic Co-operation and
  Development (OECD) 67
  anti-bribery legislation 12, 13
  climate change 60–1
  debt sustainability 49–51
  economic growth 1–2
  financial flows 4
  interest groups 16–17
  investment standards 56
  manufacturing markets 35
  natural resources 6
  ODA 43–7
  remittance innovations 57–8
  trade preference schemes 27–9, 32–3
outsourcing 22

pan-OECD anti-bribery legislation 12, 13
partnerships 52
payment in kind 10
peasant agriculture 65
peer-matching exercises 53
per capita income 1–2, 39
performance–returns link 51–2
'permanent income' approach 15
public financial management performance
  reports 45
'photogenic' aid use 6
pipeline project 14–15
plant adaptation 62
policy implementation
  economic growth 2
  food security 64–5
  investment capacity 53–4
  manufacturing 21, 25–6, 30
  strategic policies 3–4
political economy 27–8, 36, 37
population growth 37–8
poverty reduction 43–4

preference schemes 19–33, 72
price changes
  capital goods 39–40
  commodities 5, 51–2
private investment 52, 53–7
procurement rules 10, 68
product concentration 24
production fragmentation 22–5, 28
productivity levels
  agricultural 64–5
  manufacturing 22–4
  regional integration 36–8
project aid 46
prospecting natural resources 5–10, 48
protectionism
  agricultural 62–3
  clustering 30
  regional markets 41–2
PSA (public service agency) 46–7
public finance assessments (PFAs) 45
public investment
  absorptive capacity 53–4
  debt sustainability 48–50
  innovations in 54–5
public–private partnerships 52
public service agency (PSA) 46–7
pump-priming schemes 31–2

Qiaotou city 24, 27

regional integration 4, 35–42, 71–2
relative income differentials 1
relocation inducements 26–7
remittance innovations 57–8
rents 5, 7–8, 19–20
returns
  diminishing 20
  increasing 23–4
  performance link 51–2
revenues
  centralisation 11–12
  commodity price effects 5
  saving/investing 14–15
risks
  commercial borrowing 50–1
  environmental 11
  foreign equity 56–7
  global food shocks 64–5
  guide 1
  investment risks 9, 23, 40–1, 55

small economies 39
rules of origin (ROOs) 19, 22, 28–31
Russia 59

savings funds 14–15
scale economies 35
scale thresholds
   clustering 23–4
   manufacturing exports 20–1
sectoral adaptation 63–4
service providers 46–7
shocks, climatic 59, 64–5
skills acquisition 23
small economies' integration 38–41
social outcomes of aid 47
soft infrastructure 71
sovereign wealth funds (SWFs) 16, 57
spatial concentration 24–5
specialisation 30–1
Spence, Michael 17, 48
splitting value chain 22
standards
   investment 55–6
   natural resources 15, 17
strategic policies 3–4
structure costs 54
subsidies 27
supply response, trade preferences 20–1
sustainable debt 48–52
SWFs *see* sovereign wealth funds

Tanzania 27
tariff removal schemes 26
taxation
   concessions 31

remittances 58
systems 6–10, 31, 49, 58
technological externalities 23
temporary migration 58
thin markets 40–1
threshold effects 20–1, 23–4, 25
time-consistency problem 8, 55
trade preferences 19–33, 72
transparency mechanisms 12, 17
transport sector 39

unbundling 22
UNIDO proposal, 2009 32
United States of America (USA)
   global food shocks 64
   trade preference schemes 19, 29, 72
urbanisation 36–8, 69
   see also city size
USA *see* United States of America

violence 11–12
voluntary norms 17

wellbeing indicators 1
West Africa 26
World Bank 44, 50–2, 57, 70
World Trade Organization (WTO)
   corporate corruption 13–14
   government commitments 9
   local content procurement rules 10, 68
   trade preference schemes 32

Yemen 48

Zoellick, Robert 57